HOME MORTGAGE LAW PRIMER

Second Edition

Revised and Updated by

Margaret C. Jasper, Esq.

Oceana's Legal Almanac Series:
Law for the Layperson

2000
Oceana Publications, Inc.
Dobbs Ferry, N.Y.

You may order this or any other Oceana publications by visiting Oceana's Web Site at http://www.oceanalaw.com

Library of Congress Cataloging-in-Publication Data

Jasper, Margaret C.
    Home mortgage law primer / by Margaret C. Jasper.—2nd ed.
       p. cm.— (Oceana's legal almanac series. Law for the layperson, ISSN 1075-7376)
    Rev. ed. of : Home mortgage law primer / Mavis Fowler. 1995.
    ISBN 0-379-11338-4 cloth: (alk. paper)
      1. Morgages—United States—Popular works. 2. Mortgage loans—Law and legislation—United States—Popular works.
    I. Fowler, Mavis. Home mortgage law primer. II. Title. III. Series.
    KF695.Z9 F69 2000
    346.7304'364—dc21   99-56649

Oceana's Legal Almanac Series: Law for the Layperson
ISSN 1075-7376

Manufactured in the United States of America on acid-free paper.

To My Husband Chris

**Your love and support
are my motivation and inspiration**

-and-

In memory of my son, Jimmy

ABOUT THE AUTHOR

MARGARET C. JASPER is an attorney engaged in the general practice of law in South Salem, New York, concentrating in the areas of personal injury and entertainment law. Ms. Jasper holds a Juris Doctor degree from Pace University School of Law, White Plains, New York, is a member of the New York and Connecticut bars, and is certified to practice before the United States District Courts for the Southern and Eastern Districts of New York, and the United States Supreme Court. Ms. Jasper has been appointed to the panel of arbitrators of the American Arbitration Association and the law guardian panel for the Family Court of the State of New York, is a member of the Association of Trial Lawyers of America, and is a New York State licensed real estate broker and member of the Westchester County Board of Realtors, operating as Jasper Real Estate, in South Salem, New York.

Ms. Jasper is the author and general editor of the following legal almanacs: Juvenile Justice and Children's Law; Marriage and Divorce; Estate Planning; The Law of Contracts; The Law of Dispute Resolution; Law for the Small Business Owner; The Law of Personal Injury; Real Estate Law for the Homeowner and Broker; Everyday Legal Forms; Dictionary of Selected Legal Terms; The Law of Medical Malpractice; The Law of Product Liability; The Law of No-Fault Insurance; The Law of Immigration; The Law of Libel and Slander; The Law of Buying and Selling; Elder Law; The Right to Die; AIDS Law; The Law of Obscenity and Pornography; The Law of Child Custody; The Law of Debt Collection; Consumer Rights Law; Bankruptcy Law for the Individual Debtor; Victim's Rights Law; Animal Rights Law; Workers' Compensation Law; Employee Rights in the Workplace; Probate Law; Environmental Law; Labor Law; The Americans with Disabilities Act; The Law of Capital Punishment; Education Law; The Law of Violence Against Women; Landlord-Tenant Law; Insurance Law; Religion and the Law; Commercial Law; Motor Vehicle Law; Social Security Law; The Law of Drunk Driving; The Law of Speech and the First Amendment; Employment Discrimination Under Title VII; and Hospital Liability Law.

TABLE OF CONTENTS

INTRODUCTION

Owning one's home is the American dream. Home ownership carries with it a multitude of benefits generally not available to those who lease or rent. For example, owning a home is often less expensive than renting property, and ownership affords tax deductions which are not available to the renter. There is also long-term security and flexibility in home ownership whereas a renter is subject to the landlord's requirements. In addition, the value of property generally increases even as the value of paper money decreases.

Nevertheless, most Americans do not have the financial means to purchase a home outright in a cash transaction. Thus, one of the biggest obstacles one faces in realizing this dream is financing the purchase of a home. This is generally accomplished by obtaining a home mortgage from a bank or other real estate lender.

This legal almanac discusses, among other things, the history and concept of mortgaging property, the sources of real estate financing, the types of mortage devices available, mortgage interest considerations, foreclosure proceedings, and illegal real estate financing practices. This almanac also provides the reader with a basic guide to the mortgage loan process and the final closing of the real estate transaction.

The Appendix provides resource directories and other pertinent information and data. The Glossary contains definitions of many of the terms used throughout the almanac.

CHAPTER 1
HISTORICAL DEVELOPMENT OF
REAL ESTATE FINANCE

English Background

Although the concept of mortgage can be traced back to the Roman Empire, American mortgage law developed in large part from early English common law, both in its substance and terminology. The common law mortgage that developed in England during the 14th and 15th centuries involved a deed of a defeasible fee from the mortgagor to the mortgagee.

Law Day

The mortgage set forth a repayment date, known as "law day." If the mortgagor satisfied the debt on or before law day, the mortgagee's estate ended and the mortgagor regained title to the land. If the mortgagor was unable to satisfy the debt on or before law day, the defeasible fee became a fee simple absolute—i.e., ownership which is absolute, lasts forever and exists without any limitations or conditions—and the mortgagor forfeited all rights and title to the land. This was an absolute rule which was strictly applied even if the mortgagor could not locate the mortgagee to pay him.

The Equity of Redemption

Recognizing the harshness of this law, particularly on the mortgagor, the courts of equity—known as the English Chancery—intervened to assist the mortgagor who failed to make payment on law day. If the mortgagor could establish certain equitable grounds for relief such as fraud, accident, misrepresentation, or duress, the equity courts would permit the mortgagor to redeem the land upon payment of the debt even though law day had passed.

Eventually, the granting of this equitable relief of late payment became so routine that the mortgagor no longer needed to establish the specific equitable grounds for relief. This right to late redemption was referred to as the mortgagor's "equity of redemption," and was recognized as an equitable estate in land.

Right of Strict Foreclosure

This permissive right of redemption distressed the mortgagees who feared that mortgagors would now choose to delay satisfying their debt by law day, and instead sue in equity to redeem their property regardless of their late payment.

In order to address these concerns, the equity courts gave the mortgagee a right to foreclose. Thus, after the mortgagor either failed to pay the debt on law day, or to bring a suit to redeem the property, the mortgagee could request the equity court to order the mortgagor to pay the debt, interest and costs within a fixed period. Failure to comply with the court decree meant that the mortgagor's right to redeem was forever barred.

This type of foreclosure, which is rarely used today, is known as strict foreclosure under which the land is not sold but forfeited to the mortgagee regardless of its value in relation to the original mortgage debt. The mortgagee is given a fee simple absolute.

American Developments

The colonists came to America in pursuit of their dream of absolute ownership of a piece of the New World. The restrictiveness of land ownership under the English common law was not acceptable to them, and was a major cause of the colonial revolt.

The Allodial System

This dissatisfaction led to a form of land ownership in the United States known as the allodial system. Under the allodial system, the titled owner of the property owns it absolutely, subject to the restrictions set forth by the established laws and regulations which govern real estate ownership in America.

Foreclosure by Sale

Although "strict foreclosure" has been used in a minority of states, the primary method of foreclosure in the United States involves a public sale of the property. Generally, the mortgagor cannot lose his "equity of redemption" unless there has been a valid foreclosure of the mortgage. This is so even if the mortgage is in substantial default. Thus, no agreement of the parties to the mortgage, or contemporaneous with it, can cut off a recalcitrant mortgagor's rights in the mortgaged property without the mortgagee resorting to foreclosure. This concept has been referred to as "the prohibition against clogging the mortgagor's equity of redemption."

There are two methods by which a property may be sold in foreclosure: (i) judicial foreclosure; and (ii) power of sale foreclosure.

Judicial Foreclosure

A "judicial foreclosure" refers to a public sale which is held after a judicial proceeding takes place. All of the persons interested in the property must be named as parties to the proceeding. In many states this is the sole method of foreclosure because its court supervision provision provides the utmost protection to the mortgagor. Unfortunately, it is time-consuming and expensive to pursue.

Power of Sale Foreclosure

A "power of sale foreclosure" refers to a public sale which takes place after there has been some form of notice to the parties without the requirement of a judicial proceeding. A power of sale foreclosure is generally available only where the mortgage instrument—generally known as a "deed of trust"—contains a provision which gives the mortgagee the "power" to sell the property without judicial supervision.

Statutory Redemption

Many states provide the mortgagor with a statutory redemption period after the equity of redemption has been effectively cut off by a valid foreclosure sale during which time the mortgagor may redeem the land by paying the foreclosure sale price. Depending on the jurisdiction, the statutory redemption period ranges from a few months in some states to as long as 15 months in a few others. Statutory redemption was designed to encourage high bidding at the original sale. Thus, to implement this objective, the redemption amount is usually the sale price and not the mortgage debt.

The topic of foreclosure is discussed further in Chapter 7 of this almanac.

Balloon Note Mortgages

Until the 1930s, most mortgages were of the "balloon-note" type. The periodic payments made under a balloon note mortgage are generally only applied to interest. Thus, at the end of the loan term the debtor must pay the entire principal in one "balloon" payment.

Typically, during the 1930s, balloon note mortgages were of short-term duration—e.g., three or five year terms—which gave mortgagors little time to save the entire principal that became due. Nevertheless, a borrower who was unable to pay the entire balloon payment on its due date was generally able to renew the note or refinance it with another lender.

Following the depression, lenders were in desperate need for cash. For example, savings and loans associations (S&Ls) were receiving less savings because of the high unemployment rate. Consequently, many lenders had to demand full payment and foreclose on properties when mortgagors could not pay. As further discussed below, Congress responded to this disastrous financial situation with many sweeping legislative changes.

The National Housing Act of 1934

The National Housing Act of 1934 created the Federal Housing Administration (FHA) which introduced mortgage insurance and popularized the amortized mortgage loan system under which mortgagors were permitted to repay loans over many years. Today most mortgages are amortized or repaid over a substantial number of years.

Amortization is the periodic reduction of principal so that the borrower, when making his last regular payment, will have reduced his mortgage balance to zero. Each periodic payment of an amortized mortgage loan includes the interest as well as principal of the loan.

Federal Home Loan Bank System (FHLB)

Historically, the S&Ls provided a great deal of the financing for middle class urban homes prior to the depression. However, S&Ls experienced a liquidity crisis during the 1930s. In an effort to help save the S&Ls, Congress created the Federal Home Loan Bank System (FHLB) in 1932.

Federal Savings and Loan Insurance Corporation (FSLIC)

Further, in order to insure the safety of deposits in S&Ls, Congress authorized the creation of the Federal Savings and Loan Insurance Corporation (FSLIC) under the authority of Title IV of the National Housing Act of 1934.

Financial Institutions Reform, Recovery and Enforcement Act (FIRREA)

Like the S&Ls during the depression, the S&Ls of the 1980s experienced numerous difficulties and consequently, many failed. One of the reasons for their failure during the 1980s is that they held low-yield, fixed-rate mortgages during periods of high inflation. Since that time, there have been many innovations made to protect S&Ls from such risks.

One such modification was the enactment of the Financial Institutions Reform, Recovery and Enforcement Act (FIRREA) in 1989, which completely changed how S&Ls are regulated. FIRREA abolished the Federal Home Loan Bank Board (FHLBB) which was replaced by the Office of Thrift Supervision (OTS) under the Treasury Department. FIRREA did not, however, get rid of the regional Federal Home Loan Banks.

After the enactment of FIRREA, deposits in savings institutions were insured up to $100,000 by the Savings Association Insurance Fund (SAIF). SAIF is part of the Federal Deposit Insurance Corporation (FDIC), whose powers to ensure the safety of financial institutions also include supervision of bank deposit insurance funds (BIF). FIRREA significantly also created the Resolution Trust Corporation (RTC) to get rid of failed S&Ls along with their assets.

CHAPTER 2
MORTGAGE DEVICES

In General

A mortgage involves the transfer of a real estate interest by a mortgagor to a mortgagee as security for payment of a debt. A mortgagor ("borrower") is one who borrows money and, in return, gives a mortgage or deed of trust on real property as security to the mortgagee ("lender"). In most instances, an individual is the mortgagor and a bank or mortgage company is the mortgagee.

The mortgage represents the mortgagee's security interest in the real estate. The mortgage remains as a "lien" on the property until the underlying debt is paid in full. The mortgagee usually retains a "first mortgage" on the property, which generally gives the mortgagee the first right to the property if the mortgagor defaults.

The basic mortgage is a two-party instrument between the mortgagor and mortgagee which is similar to a deed. It contains words of grant and a description of the mortgaged land. Like a contract, a mortgage has certain requirements which must be satisfied in order for it to be valid. The parties must be competent and of legal age to enter into the mortgage. Further, the mortgage must be in writing and signed by all of the parties who have an interest in the property.

Depending on the jurisdiction, the mortgage must be sealed, witnessed and "delivered." The mortgage is normally considered to be "delivered" when the mortgagor releases control over it with the intent of making it operative.

Since most lenders require that the mortgage be recorded to perfect their lien and to protect their interest from subsequent creditors and purchasers, it should also be acknowledged, i.e., signed before a notary public. The mortgage is then usually recorded expeditiously following its execution by filing it in the office of land records in the county where the property is situated along with the required fee.

When the mortgage debt has been paid in full, the mortgagee executes a release of lien, also generally known as a release deed, satisfaction or discharge of a mortgage debt, depending on the jurisdiction. The release of lien is filed in the office of land records so that the existing mortgage lien of record may be removed.

Real Estate Lien

As stated above, the mortgage is represented as a "lien" on the property in which the mortgagee has a security interest. A lien is basically defined as a charge or encumbrance on property for the satisfaction of a debt or other obligation. In the case of real property, liens generally occur in one of the following ways:

1. A lien may arise by an agreement between the owner and other parties. Thus, an owner may agree to place a lien on real property in order to obtain mortgage financing to purchase the property. This is typically the manner in which real property is purchased.

2. A lien may arise when a contractor does work on the property. This is known as a "mechanic's lien."

3. A lien may also result due to unpaid obligations of the property owner, as follows:

(a) The law usually permits a judgment creditor to file their judgment in the land records so that it becomes a lien on the debtor's real property, even though the debt is unrelated to the property. The judgment creditor may then collect the debt by either foreclosing on the lien thus forcing a sale, or waiting until the debtor wishes to sell the property at which time all liens and encumbrances must be satisfied in order to give a clear title to the new owner.

(b) Unpaid property taxes may become a lien on the property.

(c) Unpaid federal and state taxes, such as income tax, sales taxes, and the like, may also become a lien on the taxpayer's real property if the taxing authorities undertake certain procedures

(d) Depending upon state law, unpaid child support may be a lien on real property

(e) The court in a matrimonial case may award one spouse ownership of the marital home, but grant the other spouse a lien on the property to the extent of the spouse's interest in the property at the time of the divorce.

If the debtor sells the property without satisfying a lien, the lien is not discharged and may still be satisfied by a sale of the property, even after it has been sold to a new owner. Thus, in practice, a purchaser will generally not buy property that is encumbered by liens. Further, a bank or other mortgage lender will generally not provide mortgage financing until all liens on the property have been removed.

Sale of Mortgaged Property

The fact that the lender has a security interest in the property does not preclude the owner from selling the property. Nevertheless, the mortgage amount must be satisfied as a condition of the sale. The proceeds of the sale are used to satisfy the outstanding mortgage.

Sold Subject to Mortgage

If the property were to be sold without the debt being satisfied, then the buyer would be accepting the property "subject to" the existing mortgage. This means that the lender retains its security interest in the property even though there is a different owner. The seller also remains personally liable for payment of the debt.

Assumption of Debt

Although the buyer is not "personally" liable for the debt, because the buyer was not a party to the mortgage, the buyer can still lose the property in a foreclosure sale if the seller defaults on the mortgage payments. Nevertheless, if the buyer expressly "assumes" the existing mortgage debt, with the permission of the mortgagee, the buyer also becomes liable for the debt. In this case, the mortgagee may collect the outstanding debt from either the seller or the buyer.

Substitution

The seller is not relieved from its obligation under the mortgage unless the mortgagee expressly agrees to "substitute" the buyer for the seller. However, because substitution lessens the mortgagee's remedies should there be a default, it is not commonly done.

Theories of Title and Possession

There has been much uncertainty regarding the nature of the mortgagee's interest in the mortgaged property. As discussed below, three "theories" of mortgage law exist today in the United States which address the issue of possession.

Title Theory

The title theory has its roots in the English common law. Under this theory, legal "title" and the right to possession is always in the mortgagee until the mortgage has been satisfied or foreclosed. However, those jurisdictions which still adhere to the common law "title" theory consider the mortgagee's "title" as simply that of holding a security interest.

Intermediate Theory

According to the intermediate theory, the mortgage does not convey title to the mortgagee but instead creates a security interest. The intermediate theory gives the right to possession to the mortgagor, at least until default, and, generally to the mortgagee after default.

Lien Theory

The majority of states subscribe to the lien theory, which provides that the mortgage does not convey legal title to the mortgagee, but gives the mortgagee a lien on the property. The mortgagor generally retains the right to possession until a foreclosure.

Conventional Mortgages

Loans usually fall under the categories of conventional mortgages or governmental mortgages. A conventional mortgage is one which is made directly by the lender to the buyer with very few regulations or restrictions. Following are commonly used mortgage devices.

Purchase Money Mortgage

Where a mortgagee finances a mortgagor's acquisition of mortgaged real estate, the mortgage is known as a purchase-money mortgage. Although traditionally, a purchase-money mortgage referred to a mortgage taken by the seller of the real estate as security for the loan, a mortgage given by a third party lending institution is now also generally considered to be a purchase-money mortgage.

Sellers often used purchase money mortgages to finance the sale without involving a financial institution in order to reduce federal income taxes. Thus, if part of the purchase price is received in future years, the seller can treat the transaction as an installment sale and count as income only that portion of the profit represented by the year's payments. This device defers the tax due and may place the seller in a lower tax bracket by reducing income received in any one year.

During times of tight mortgage markets, sellers are often compelled to agree to finance the transaction in order to sell the property. If mortgage funds are not easily available or are only available at very high interest rates, buyers will seek alternate sources of funds. Sellers who are financially able to carry a purchase-money mortgage make their properties more attractive by providing this alternative source of financing.

When the transaction involves vacant, unimproved land—known as "raw" land—a purchase-money mortgage frequently contains a subordination clause to allow the purchaser to obtain a first mortgage loan to finance the building of improvements on the property. In that case, the purchase-money mortgage becomes a "junior" mortgage, which is more fully discussed below.

Non-Purchase Money Mortgage

If the mortgagee lends money on real estate already owned by the mortgagor, the mortgage is known as a non-purchase money mortgage. A common example of a non-purchase-money mortgage is a second mortgage that a long-time homeowner gives to a lending institution on his or her home to secure a loan.

Deed of Trust

A deed of trust is generally defined as a mortgage with a "power of sale" provision. In some states, the deed of trust is considered a mortgage, and in other states it is considered to be "in the nature" of a mortgage. The deed of trust is a three-party instrument among a grantor—i.e., the mortgagor;—a trustee; and a beneficiary—the mortgagee/lender. The appointed trustee is the individual or entity to whom the conveyance of real property is made as security for the loan. The trustee may be the mortgagee's agent, although an impartial third party is preferable and often required.

The difference between a conventional mortgage and a deed of trust lies in the manner in which the lender can enforce the provisions of the deed should the borrower default in payment of the loan. The deed of trust permits the trustee, at the request of the beneficiary/mortgagee, to foreclose on the property by power of sale—i.e., a sale which takes place generally without court supervision. Thus, a deed of trust instrument must contain an appointed trustee, a trust clause, and a power of sale clause.

If the deed of trust is used as a mortgage, it normally contains a defeasance clause which renders the deed of trust void upon payment of the debt. However, because the title record still needs to be cleared of the lien, the beneficiary/mortgagee usually executes a release of lien.

If the deed of trust is used "in the nature" of a mortgage, upon full payment of the note, the trustee generally executes a "deed of reconveyance," or "release deed," which reconveys whatever title the trustee may have had back to the grantor/mortgagor.

Junior Mortgages

Because a mortgage represents a security interest in land, a mortgagor is free to mortgage his property to as many lenders as are willing to make the loans. The placing of a second, third or even fourth mortgage on property is called "secondary financing." Such secondary and subsequent mortgages are categorized as junior mortgages.

Lenders enter into these junior mortgages only if the mortgagor has enough "equity" in the property. The mortgagor's equity is the difference between the current market value of the property and the total debt obligations against the property, including any prior mortgage loans.

A junior mortgage involves a relatively high risk because the secondary lender's security interest extends only to the value of the property in excess of prior liens. Therefore, lenders generally make junior mortgage loans for a shorter term and at a higher interest rate than first mortgage loans.

Reverse Mortgage

A reverse mortgage loan pays a homeowner monthly cash advances or provides the homeowner with a line of credit by converting the homeowner's equity into cash. A reverse mortgage does not require repayment for as long as the borrower lives in the home. However, because the homeowner is drawing on the value of the home, there will be less equity available for the homeowner or his or her heirs in the future.

Interest rates on a reverse mortgage may be higher and are charged on a compound basis. Application fees, discount points and closing costs may also be higher than other types of loans. Further, interest rates are not tax deductible until the loan is repaid in full.

Because of the complex nature of reverse mortgages, the reader is advised to seek the advice of a financial advisor, real estate attorney or accountant before entering into the loan agreement.

Government Mortgages

Unlike the conventional mortgage, government mortgages may contain strict restrictions on the mortgage terms and conditions. The most commonly sought governmental mortgages include the Federal Housing Administration (FHA) mortgages, which are insured, and the Veterans Administration (VA) mortgages, which are guaranteed.

FHA Mortgages

Under an FHA mortgage, the FHA insures the loan which is actually made by a private lender. This is an incentive for the lender to make the loan, particularly since FHA mortgages call for much lower downpayments, e.g. 95 to 97% loan to value financing. The FHA retains certain controls over approval of the mortgage. For example, the FHA makes its own appraisal of the property to make sure it meets their minimum standards. The FHA also places maximum limits on the mortgage amounts.

A list of FHA closing requirements is set forth at Appendix 1.

VA Mortgage

Under the VA mortgage program, lenders are refunded the full amount of the guaranteed portion of the loan if the veteran defaults. The VA also requires its own appraisal of the property prior to the loan being made.

Secondary Market Mortgages

The government has also created a secondary mortgage market in which they buy first mortgages from various lenders. This frees the lender's finances so that they can make additional loans, and serves the public interest, particularly when the economic climate is not good.

The most common secondary market purchasers are the Federal National Mortgage Association (FNMA)—commonly known as "Fannie Mae," the Government National Mortgage Association (GNMA)—commonly known as "Ginnie Mae," and the Federal Home Loan Mortgage Corporation (FHLMC)— commonly known as "Freddie Mac." Each particular purchaser has their own rules and requirements concerning the mortgages they are willing to buy.

Late Payment Clauses

To assist the mortgagee in receiving timely payments and to avoid the problems of collecting payments after the agreed upon mortgage payment deadlines pass, late payment clauses are usually included in mortgage documents, promissory notes, or both. Late payment clauses enable the mortgagee to charge a late fee for payments received a certain number of days after the due date.

The purpose of the late payment fee is to cover the bookkeeping expenses of having to post late payments. Late payment fees are legal in all types of loans. A typical late payment clause provides as follows:

If any payment due is received later than fifteen days after the due date of the payment, a late charge of [xx%] percent of the amount then overdue may be charged by the mortgagee for the purpose of defraying costs of collection and posting of the account.

Due-on-Sale Clause

A "due-on-sale" clause, also known as a "call" clause, provides that the mortgagor may not convey the property to another party without first paying off the note or renegotiating the interest rate. The due-on-sale clause gives the mortgagee the right to "call" the entire balance of an indebtedness due and payable if the borrower sells the mortgaged property.

Due-on-sale clauses may eliminate an important incentive for buyers to purchase mortgaged property, particularly where the interest rate on the current mortgage is substantially lower than that available on new mortgage loans.

On the other hand, due-on-sale clauses protect lenders by giving them an opportunity to make a new loan on terms which are more favorable to them. The following is a typical due-on-sale clause:

TRANSFER OF THE PROPERTY; ASSUMPTION: If all or any part of the property or an interest therein is sold or transferred by Borrower without Lender's prior consent, excluding: (a) the creation of a lien or encumbrance subordinate to this deed of trust; (b) the creation of a purchase money security interest for household appliances; (c) transfer by devise, descent, or by operation of law upon the death of a joint tenant; or (d) the grant of any leasehold interest of three years or less not containing an option to purchase, the Lender may, at the Lender's option, declare all sums secured by this Deed of Trust to be immediately due and payable. Lender shall have waived such option to accelerate if, prior to the sale or transfer, Lender and the person to whom the property is to be sold or transferred reach agreement in writing that the credit of such person is satisfactory to Lender and that the interest payable on the sums secured by this Deed of Trust shall be at such rate as the Lender shall request. If Lender has waived the option to accelerate provided in this paragraph, and if the Borrower's successor in interest has executed a written assumption agreement accepted by Lender, Lender shall release Borrower from all obligations under this Deed of Trust and Note. If Lender exercises the option to accelerate, Lender shall mail Borrower notice of such acceleration at least 30 days prior to the time Lender will declare such sums due and payable.

Due-on-sale clauses are viewed very differently by lenders and borrowers. In inflationary times, lenders view due-on-sale clauses as necessary for their economic security. At the same time, borrowers see due-on-sale clauses as unfair, as an unreasonable restraint on title transfer opportunities, and as an attempt to "gouge" the public for purely economic reasons.

This basic difference of opinion between lenders and borrowers has resulted in extensive litigation. Some states tend to favor automatic enforcement of the "due-on-sale" clause, while others tend not to approve this clause unless a mortgage assumption results in a material detriment to the security interest. However, all states tend to look for equitable and just results when the case merits it. There are so many exceptions and extreme fact situations that many of the due-on-sale litigations are determined on a case-by-case basis.

Some states have attempted to define their position by statute, but this also created conflicts. In an early effort to remedy these inconsistencies between states, Congress passed the Garn-St. Germain Depository Institutions Act of 1982. A provision of this statute addresses the federal government's preemption of state laws prohibiting enforcement of due-on-sale clauses.

This federal preemption was reinforced in *Fidelity Federal Savings and Loan Association v. De la Cuesta*, 102 S.Ct. 3014 (1982). In *Fidelity*, the court held that the preemption can override state laws because it is enabled by the Supremacy Clause of the United States Constitution (Article VI, Clause 2. Thus, federal law will control over any contravening state law.

An exception to the statute exists whereby a state may enact a law that exempts that state from the application of the Garn-St. Germain preemption in connection with loans originated in that state by lenders other than national banks. This exception allows a state to preempt the federal preemption.

If there is a loan secured by a lien on residential real property of one to four dwelling units, under Garn-St.Germain, a lender may not exercise his option pursuant to a due-on-sale clause upon the following items:

1. The creation of a lien or other encumbrance subordinate to the lender's security instrument which does not relate to the transfer of rights of occupancy in the property;

2. The creation of a purchase money security interest for household appliances;

3. A transfer by devise, dissent, or operation of law on the death of a joint tenant or a tenant by the entirety;

4. A leasehold interest of three years or less, not containing an option to purchase;

5. A transfer where the spouse or the children of the borrower become owner(s) of the property;

6. A transfer resulting from a decree of dissolution of a marriage, legal separation agreement, or from an incidental property settlement agreement, by which the spouse of the borrower becomes an owner of the property;

7. A transfer to a relative resulting from the death of the borrower; and

8. A transfer into an inter vivos trust in which the borrower is and remains a beneficiary and which does not relate to a transfer of rights of occupancy in the property; or any other transfer of disposition described in regulations prescribed by the Federal Home Loan Bank Board.

The Act also provides an encouragement clause that requires national banks to blend the previous rate with the current rate. Prepayment penalties may not be imposed by the lenders when exercising their due-on-transfer clauses. The acceleration of the indebtedness eliminates prepayment.

Many lawyers and brokers have attempted to get around the due-on-sale clauses by redefining the "transfer" of the property so it would not constitute a sale. According to the Federal Home Loan Bank Board (FHLBB) rules, however, these attempts to get around the due-on-sale clauses will probably not be effective.

Under FHLBB rules, a "sale or transfer" includes the conveyance of real property or any right, title or interest therein whether legal or equitable, whether voluntary or involuntary, by outright sale, deed, installment sale contract, land contract, contract for deed, lease-hold interest with a term greater than three years, lease option contract, or any other method of conveyance of real property interest."

Transfer of the Mortgagor's Interest

The owner-mortgagor may always convey the mortgaged property. A mortgage provision attempting to prevent conveyance is void as an illegal restraint on alienation.

When a mortgagor conveys the mortgaged property, it is important to determine whether the mortgage is discharged before title passes or survives the conveyance. This depends upon the agreement or contract between the mortgagor and his grantee.

If an owner's mortgage does not contain a "due-on-sale" clause, there are two methods by which property can be conveyed without having to change the terms of, or pay off, the original mortgage note. One method involves an assumption of the mortgagor's existing indebtedness; the second involves buying the property "subject to" the existing indebtedness.

Assumption of Mortgage

If a loan is "assumed," the grantee of the property becomes primarily liable on the note and mortgage, while the grantor acts as a surety in case the note is not paid in full. If there is a default on the note, the lender must pursue his remedy against the grantee first. If the grantee cannot satisfy the indebtedness, the lender may then sue the original grantor as the original signatory on the note and mortgage. Thus, even though the grantor sells his property, he or she may yet be liable on the note at some later date should the buyer default on the payments.

Sale "Subject To" Existing Mortgage

When property is sold "subject to" an existing mortgage, the grantee does not become personally obligated to pay off the mortgage but merely has the option of paying off the mortgage if he so chooses. The grantor remains primarily liable on the note and the grantee has no obligation at all to the original lender. This represents a type of nonrecourse financing because it does not personally obligate the purchaser to pay the existing mortgage.

As discussed above, if there is a "due-on-sale" clause in the original mortgage, an assumption of mortgage normally cannot take effect until the subsequent grantee has been approved by the lender. However, in the "subject to" transaction, there is some uncertainty as to whether it requires the approval of the lender before such a conveyance can take place. This is because the lender's security is not impaired insofar as the original mortgagor remains primarily liable on the note unlike an assumption.

CHAPTER 3
MORTGAGE INTEREST CONSIDERATIONS

In General

Interest is a charge paid by the borrower to the lender for the use of the lender's money. A lender will charge a borrower a certain percentage of the principal as interest for each year the debt is outstanding. The amount of interest due on any one installment payment date is generally calculated by computing the total yearly interest based on the unpaid balance and dividing that figure by the number of payments made each year.

Interest is customarily due and charged at the end of each payment period, e.g. monthly or quarterly, etc. This is known as "payment in arrears." Since mortgage loan payments are generally made on a monthly basis, the interest portion of each payment covers the charge for using the borrowed money during the previous month. Some lenders specify in the mortgage note that interest is charged in advance, however, for practical purposes, the distinction only matters when and if the property is sold before the debt is repaid.

Fixed Rate Amortized Mortgage

The most common mortgage is the fixed rate amortized mortgage. Under a fixed rate amortized mortgage, the loan amount generally bears interest at a fixed percentage rate per year. This means that the rate does not change and thus there is a set monthly payment over the entire term of the loan, e.g. 30 years. Each monthly payment consists of both principal and interest.

In the early years of the loan, the interest is usually the larger share of the payment. As the loan term comes to a close, the principal payment makes up the larger share of the payment. At the end of the loan period, the entire principal and interest debt is repaid.

A mortgage payment estimation chart is set forth at Appendix 2.

During the Great Depression, new programs such as FHA mortgage insurance led to widespread use of the long-term fixed interest rate mortgage, which has been the standard for more than six decades. Nevertheless, an extended maturity is not completely to the borrower's advantage. The longer a loan term is, the longer it takes for equity to build, which inevitably translates into larger total interest charges.

In fact, many state statutes have, until recently, limited the maximum loan amortization period to 30 years. Despite this there is a trend to increase the maximum permissible term to 35 and even 40 years.

Adjustable Rate Mortgage

Many people seek to lock in low interest rates with a fixed rate mortgage. However, in years when inflation is high, a low interest fixed rate mortgage provides the lender with less of a yield than anticipated on the loan. Over the years, lenders became increasingly dissatisfied with the diminished returns on fixed rate mortgages. This led to the development of alternative mortgage instruments, such as the adjustable rate mortgage (ARM).

An adjustable rate mortgage, also known as a variable rate mortgage (VRM), does not have a fixed payment. The interest rate under an ARM is subject to periodic adjustment up or down at various intervals during the loan term—e.g., every 1, 3 or 5 years. The interest rate is gauged by the movement of a specified standard, such as the existing prime rate at the time of adjustment.

A sample Adjustable Rate Note is set forth at Appendix 3.

A variable rate mortgage may provide for balloon payments. This means that, although the loan is amortized over a longer period of time, e.g. thirty years, for the purpose of calculating a monthly payment, the loan actually becomes due and payable after a shorter period of time, such as five years, at which time the balloon payment—the entire indebtedness—must be paid.

If the ARM's interest rate increases are added to the principal of the loan, the principal balance of the loan may increase instead of decrease, depending on the rate of increase. This is known as negative amortization. More commonly, the interest rate increase extends the maturity of the loan, or is reflected in increased monthly payments.

Despite its common use in England, Canada and many other countries, the adjustable rate mortgage was not widely available in the United States until 1979, when the Federal Home Loan Bank Board (FHLBB) authorized federally chartered savings and loan associations to issue ARMs. Nevertheless, the FHLBB also required the Savings and Loan Associations (S&Ls) to continue to offer fixed-rate mortgages, which consumers preferred.

In 1980, the FHLBB authorized the S&Ls to issue renegotiated-rate mortgages (RRM), also known as "rollover" mortgages, and allowed them to stop offering fixed interest rate loans. Under this plan, home loans could be made for a term of thirty years but would "roll over" every three to five years at a renegotiated interest rate.

Although the renegotiated rate mortgage has been used for some time in several jurisdictions—e.g.,Wisconsin. Ohio, Florida, Washington and New England—the plan was strongly attacked by consumer groups, while vigorously defended by the savings and loan industry. Nevertheless, periods characterized by volatile shifts in interest rates are likely to see the use of a range of these variable-rate mortgages, such as the renegotiated-rate concept.

Graduated Payment Mortgage

The graduated payment mortgage uses the same interest rate as in a standard fixed rate mortgage, however, the monthly payments start out low and gradually increase until they rise above the level at which the standard mortgage would have been at the stage in the mortgage term. In effect, because the initial payments are not sufficient to amortize the loan, the mortgagor is borrowing the difference between the payments and the current interest, and paying off these amounts in later years.

The graduated payment mortgage concept is based upon the assumption that a family's income will increase over time and therefore the amount of income available to make payments on a home will also increase. It is particularly attractive to families who are just starting out who may have difficulty making the monthly payments required under a conventional fixed-rate mortgage during the first few years of the loan's life.

The graduated payment mortgage has three positive features:

1. It qualifies more potential homeowners for conventional loans;
2. It qualifies buyers to enter the housing market sooner; and
3. It qualifies buyers to purchase more house and amenities.

Graduated Payment Adjustable Mortgage

A variation of the graduated payment mortgage that includes the concept of variable interest rates is the graduated payment adjustable mortgage. As with the graduated payment mortgage, the initial payments are lower, however, they have the potential to increase substantially. The interest rate is generally adjustable up or down a maximum of one-half of one percentage point a year. Nevertheless, without a maximum on the "overall" increase in the interest rate, the monthly payments can rapidly increase.

For example, a thirty-year $50,000 loan at an initial rate of 13 percent can have an original payment of $428.09 a month. During the sixth year, with regular maximum interest rate increases, the monthly payment would be $657.46 whereas the payment would be $443.10 for a fixed rate mortgage at 13 percent.

Such rapid increases may create a difficult financial situation for a borrower whose income has not increased accordingly.

Split Rate Mortgage

The purpose of a split rate mortgage is to make the initial cash requirement to close more affordable for the mortgagor by financing the loan origination fee, i.e., the discount points. The points are financed by paying a higher rate of interest during the early months of the mortgage loan, e.g., the first 18 months. Thereafter, the principal and interest are adjusted to the initial commitment rate.

Basically, the borrower is paying the discount points on a monthly payment basis over the initial months of the loan rather than at the time of closing. This may be advantageous to a borrower who has little cash reserve insofar as the discount points can represent a significant portion of the closing costs, e.g., 1% to 3% of the amount of the loan.

A sample split rate mortgage clause is set forth at Appendix 4.

FLIP Mortgage

A FLIP mortgage is another graduated payment mortgage that is designed to reduce the borrower's monthly mortgage payments. The lower monthly payments are accomplished by using the borrower's down payment to fund a pledged savings account. Funds are drawn from the account each month to supplement the mortgage payment.

The pledged account also serves as additional collateral for the lender. The borrower's out-of-pocket monthly mortgage payment is less because the lender takes supplementary monthly payments from the interest-bearing pledged account funded from the borrower's down payment.

This pledged account is deposited with the lender at the time the mortgage is created. Each succeeding year, the monthly supplementary payments are reduced. In response to an individual borrower's requirements and capabilities, the FLIP mortgage takes into consideration the cost of the home, the cash available for down payment, the family income, mortgage terms and potential for income growth.

Shared Appreciation Mortgage

A Shared Appreciate Mortgage is designed to assist first- time home buyers. It has a fixed interest rate set below the prevailing market rate, along with contingent interest based on the appreciation of the property at maturity, or payment in full of the loan on sale or transfer of the property.

It is likely that the shared appreciation mortgage will be used more during periods of inflation or rising interest rates. Because the lower interest rates mean lower monthly payments, some borrowers may be more willing to purchase homes that otherwise would be beyond their reach.

The ability to buy a house that should appreciate in value may outweigh the potential appreciation given up in the form of contingent interest. The less pleasant alternative during tight money markets may be to forego the purchase because of a lack of affordable funds.

The price that must be paid for the reduced rate and payments is that the borrower will share the appreciation with the lender when the house is sold. If the borrower does not sell within ten years of obtaining a shared appreciation mortgage, then the house must either be sold or refinanced at the end of ten years. In either case, the lender collects a percentage, generally up to 40 percent of the increase in value of the home.

Buy-Down Mortgage

A buy-down mortgage is a loan whereby the borrower pays the mortgagee a substantial amount of money up front in return for a loan at below the current interest rate. The upfront money is used to offset the mortgagee's reduced rate of return on account of the lower interest rate.

Balloon Payments

As set forth above, a mortgage is generally amortized over a certain number of years, so that the full amount of the mortgage loan and the interest are paid when the term of the mortgage has expired. For example, after 30 years of a typical residential 30-year mortgage, the mortgagor will have paid the full amount of the debt and interest due on the mortgage.

When the mortgage contains a "balloon payment" clause, the result will not be the same. Under a mortgage with a balloon payment clause, the mortgagor is still required to make periodic installment payments, but those payments do not fully amortize the loan. Thus, the mortgagor will be required to pay the lump sum balance of the amount due at the end of the term of the mortgage. This lump sum is called a "balloon payment."

Prepayment Penalties

The mortgagee has the right to earn the interest on the money invested and loaned to the mortgagor for the term of the mortgage. Thus, unless the note or the mortgage specifically permits prepayment, the mortgagor has no right to prepay the amount due on the loan in advance of the mortgage term.

If the lender does not permit the mortgagor to make prepayments, the note or mortgage will generally contain a clause that requires the mortgagor to pay a penalty in order to prepay the amount due on the loan. Such a penalty is justified on the grounds that prepayment makes it necessary for the lender to find a new investment outlet and to incur the expenses associated with finding and making that reinvestment.

The prepayment penalty may apply to the entire period of the loan or may be applicable only during the first 5 to 10 years of the mortgage. A typical prepayment penalty clause provides as follows:

> In the event of default hereunder, or in the event that said mortgagor desires by reason of sale or otherwise to prepay the total amount due and owing at the time of any of the above described prepayments, the mortgagee shall have the right to assess and collect a premium of [xx%] percent of the then principal balance. The right of the mortgagee to assess and collect such premium shall continue for a period of 10 years from the time the amortization of the above described indebtedness begins.

The prepayment penalty clause is generally recognized as valid in all states. However, it should be noted that certain types of government insured loans prohibit prepayment penalties. Further, if loans are sold or transferred to certain government corporations, the loan arrangement cannot include a prepayment penalty.

CHAPTER 4
USURY

In General

Usury refers to the maximum amount of interest a lender is legally entitled to receive under a state's statute. While the principle seems fairly simple, its application to the various types of transactions in which usury may exist is relatively complex and even difficult to understand.

The doctrine of usury is approximately 2,500 years old, and had its first recorded history in the Old Testament wherein the ancient laws forbade the taking of interest against a brother, but permitted interest against a stranger. The economics of ancient Egypt and the Roman Empire were not so concerned with the taking of interest, and it was not until the Reformation and the rise of Christianity that the Old Testament view again prevailed.

The most recent usury statute adopted in England was the Statute of Anne in 1713. Under the Statute of Anne, the maximum allowable rate was set at 5 percent. If the maximum rate was exceeded, the contract was deemed void without exception.

The Statute of Anne remained in force in England for 141 years. A change in public policy occurred in 1830, when holders in due course of securities were permitted recovery even though the securities arose out of a usurious transaction. A holder in due course is one who takes an instrument for value, in good faith, and without notice that it is overdue or has been dishonored or of any defense against or claim to it on the part of any person. In 1854, England repealed all usury legislation. Since that date, the courts have resorted to the remedy of striking down unconscionable contracts.

The Statute of Anne, however, was the law in England during a critical period in American history, and served as the model for most American usury statutes. Thus, every state and the District of Columbia have usury laws in some form.

Elements

In general, the elements which constitute usury include:

1. A loan or forbearance;

2. Exaction of excessive interest; and

3. Wrongful intent.

All three elements must be present for usury to exist.

Because state usury statutes vary in their provisions, the reader is advised to check their own state's statute in this regard.

Exemptions

Recent market increases in interest rates have caused many states to consider raising or even eliminating their usury rates, and many states have provided for statutory exemptions. Exempt transactions are extremely important because, like interest rates, they impact directly on the flow of funds among the states.

For example, if residential loans are exempt from usury penalties, and the major local demand for loanable funds is for residential purchase and construction, a 6% usury rate would probably cause large amounts of loanable funds to flow out of the community to other states.

Federal Exemption

In 1980, federal laws were passed which declared that the constitutional laws of any state expressly limiting the rate or amount of interest shall not apply to any loan which is:

1. Secured by a first lien on residential property by a first lien on stock in residential cooperative housing corporations, or by a first lien on residential manufactured home;

2. Made after March 31, 1980; and

3. Described in Section 527(b) of the National Housing Act, where an individual finances the sale or exchange of residential real property which such individual owns and which such individual has occupied as his principal residence.

There is an exception that provides that the statute does not apply to any loan made in any state on or after April 1, 1983, and before April 1, 1983 if such state adopts a law or certifies that the voters of such state have voted in favor of any provision, constitutional or otherwise, which states explicitly and by its terms that such state does not want the provisions of the new federal statute to apply with respect to the loans and advances made in such state.

In interpreting the statute, the Federal Home Loan Bank Board (FHLBB) has taken the position that residential real property means real estate improved or to be improved by structures or structure designed for dwelling, as opposed to primarily commercial use. There has even been some further discussion that a wrap-around mortgage may be included as a first lien loan because of the "all-inclusive" nature of such mortgages.

The Corporate Borrower Exemption

Lenders are generally permitted to receive higher interest rates from corporate borrowers. This most important and prevalent exemption to the usury laws deprives corporate borrowers of the defense of usury on a transaction otherwise subject to the usury laws.

The corporate exemption differs in form among jurisdictions. In some states, the corporation is merely denied the defense of usury. In other states, the law applies different maximum rates to corporations as compared to individuals. Some states have no interest limitation applicable to corporations, and in other states, the corporate borrower exemption applies only if the loan exceeds a certain amount.

Sellers

Many states exempt a seller who takes back a purchase money mortgage from the buyer under the assumption that both parties to the transaction enter into the agreement from equal bargaining positions.

Penalties

In the United States, cases generally indicate that since there was no usury at common law, the governing law is statutory. Thus, one must refer to the state's usury statute to determine the applicable penalty.

Depending on the jurisdiction, a lender who charges usurious interest rates may have to forfeit all of the interest or that part of the interest which is in excess of the legal rate. Some jurisdictions further penalize the lender by taking away the lender's right to recover all or a percentage of the principal on the loan.

Treatment of Associated Financing Costs and Fees

Because there are so many costs and fees associated with mortgage loans, a lender must carefully set forth what the particular cost represents and whether it will be considered "interest" under the state's statute, and thus subject the lender to the state's usury statute.

Brokerage Fee

A brokerage fee is a charge exacted by a mortgage broker for "placing" a loan with a lender. The brokerage fee is not normally considered to be interest provided the fee does not go to the lender. Further, there can be no joint control or agreement to split the brokerage fee between the lender and the broker.

In some states and areas it is common for a mortgage company or savings and loan association to operate as a mortgage broker, charging one to five points as a fee for finding another lender to make the loan. In this capacity the mortgage company or savings and loan association is serving only as a mortgage broker. Thus, a broker's fee for finding a lender is not interest. However, fees charged by a broker who is working as a lender's agent may be considered interest.

Commitment Fee

A commitment fee is normally a fee charged for the promise of securing loan funds at some future date. It can be characterized as an option to enter into a future loan. So long as the fee is reasonably related to the risks taken by the lender, it will not be construed as interest.

Discount Points

A discount point is a charge for making the loan that is payable at the time of the loan. Each "point" represents one percent of the loan. A $100,000 loan with 2-1/2 discount points would require the borrower to pay an additional $2,500 at closing.

In some states and for some purposes, discount points are not considered interest. One test to determine if points are interest is whether they are directly attributable to expenses incurred by the lender in making the loan. If points are charged to offset a lender's expense incurred in making the loan, they do not constitute interest.

Partial Release Fees

Partial release fees may be charged when the borrower pays off part of the loan and receives clear title to a part of the mortgaged tract. These fees are normally attributable to the preparation of legal instruments, bookkeeping and clerical costs for releasing the security and resulting adjustments of the principle balance due under the terms of the loan. Partial release fees of this type are generally not considered interest.

Prepayment Penalties

Prepayment penalties are fees that a lender charges the borrower for prematurely paying off a loan. Arguably, these fees may be justified as constituting lost lender profits suffered as a result of premature payment. Conceivably, such damages could consist of additional costs incurred and/or interest payments lost.

Some courts do not construe prepayment penalties as interest, but rather as consideration for the termination of the loan contract. Others may determine that the penalties are interest if they do not bear some reasonable relationship to the amount of loss or inconvenience suffered by the lender due to prepayment.

CHAPTER 5
THE TRUTH-IN LENDING ACT

In General

The Truth-in-Lending Act was passed by Congress in 1968 as part of the Federal Consumer Protection Act. In order to carry out the basic provisions of the Act, the Federal Reserve Board promulgated specific regulations on compliance, which are referred to in their entirety as "Regulation Z," an exhaustive publication dealing with almost every imaginable area of extension of credit. This almanac addresses the provisions of the Truth-in-Lending Act that impact mortgage law.

The purpose of the Truth-in-Lending Act is to assure that everyone being extended commercial credit by a creditor covered by the Act is given meaningful disclosures regarding the cost of the credit being extended. The disclosures must be clear and according to the statutory forms published pursuant to the Act and Regulation Z.

Applicability

Regulation Z applies to all businesses and individuals who are:

1. Offering or extending credit to consumers;

2. Offering or extending such credit on a regular basis;

3. Offering or extending credit either:

(a) subject to a finance charge, or

(b) payable by written agreement in more than four installments; and

4. Offering or extending credit primarily for personal, family, or household purposes.

The types of real estate transactions that are excluded from Regulation Z coverage are as follows:

1. Business transactions;

2. Commercial transactions;

3. Agricultural transactions;

4. Organizational credit transactions; and

5. Credit transactions that involve more than $25,000 but which are not secured by real estate or a dwelling.

Disclosure

If Regulation Z is applicable to a lender in connection with a real estate transaction, then the lender is required to make certain disclosures. Generally, these disclosures are made on a statement separate from the promissory note and mortgage documents.

A sample Truth-in-Lending Act Disclosure Statement is set forth at Appendix 5.

Under Regulation Z, Section 226.4(a), the following information must be furnished to the borrower:

1. Annual percentage rate;

2. Finance charge;

3. Amount financed;

4. Total payment amount;

5. Number of payments;

6. Amount per payment;

7. Payments due date; and

8. Late payment charge.

Regulation Z defines the finance charge as ". . . [T]he sum of all charges, payable directly or indirectly by the creditor as an incident to or as a condition of the extension of credit, whether paid or payable by the customer, the seller, or any other person on behalf of the customer to the creditor or a third party."

Variable Rate Interest Loans

If the note has a variable interest rate, the following disclosure statement is also required under Regulation Z:

"The annual percentage rate may increase during the term of this transaction if the primary rate of the lender increases. The rate may not increase more often than once a year, and may not increase by more than 1% annually. The interest rate will not increase above __%. Any increase will take the form of higher payment amounts. If the interest rate increases by __ % in 1 year, your regular payment would increase to $__."

It should be noted that the regulations do not place a ceiling on the finance charges. The requirements only specify that the charges be disclosed.

Advertisements and Triggering Language

Regulation Z also restricts the manner in which lenders advertise their credit terms. Under Regulation Z, an advertisement is defined as "[A] commercial message in any media that promotes, directly or indirectly, a credit transaction."

Advertisements must be accurate and state only those terms that are actually available. Advertisements which address finance charges must also state those charges in terms of the annual percentage rate (APR)—i.e., an expression of the cost of credit according to its yearly rate. Formulas for computing the APR are set forth in the regulations, along with a table that can be used in such computation.

Regulation Z also provides that if certain "triggering language" is used in advertisements, then additional disclosures must also be included. Triggering language includes:

1. Amount or percentage of any down payment;

2. Number of payments or period of repayment;

3. Amount of any payment; and

4. Amount of any finance charge.

The additional disclosures that must be made in advertisements using triggering language include:

1. Terms of repayment;

2. Annual percentage rate; and

3. Disclosures of any increases in payments or rates that may occur.

For example, the phrase "30-year loan" is an example of a triggering term because it indicates the repayment period. The phrase "payable in monthly installments of $550" is also triggering language because it relates to the amount of the payments. Use of any of these types of "triggering" phrases requires the advertising lender to include the additional disclosures.

Nevertheless, general phrases such as "no down payment," "years to repay," and "monthly installments to suit your budget," may be used without triggering the additional disclosure requirements.

Miscellaneous Disclosures

In addition to the preceding disclosures required for real estate credit transactions, the following items must be included on the disclosure statement regardless of the type of loan or note involved:

1. Identity of the creditor;

2. Demand feature of the note, if one exists;

3. Prepayment penalties, if any;

4. Whether the loan is assignable or transferable; and

5. Separate identification of credit insurance premiums.

Right of Rescission

Although Regulation Z provides for a 3-day rescission period for security interests and second mortgages, the rescission period does not apply to residential mortgage transactions which are defined in Section 226.2(a) (24) as "[T]ransactions in which a mortgage, deed of trust, purchase money security interest arising under an installment sales contract, or equivalent consensual security interest is created or retained in the consumer's principal dwelling to finance the acquisition or initial construction of that dwelling."

Thus the exception to the 3-day rescission period and notice of that period is for first notes and mortgages on property being purchased by a consumer for use as a residence. However, the consumer who executes a second note and mortgage on a property is permitted to cancel that transaction within the 3-day period. In that case, the lender must disclose the right of cancellation and must also provide, in written form, the procedures for exercising the right of cancellation.

A sample Notice of Right to Cancel is set forth at Appendix 6.

The Truth-in-Lending Simplification and Reform Act of 1980

The Federal Truth-in-Lending Act and Regulation Z were both changed in 1980 by the Truth-in-Lending Simplification and Reform Act. This new statute became effective in 1982 and was further amended in 1983 to comply with the Depository Institutions Act of 1982. The most significant changes in the Act affecting real estate are the definitions of "creditor" and "arrangers of credit."

Under the amendments, a "creditor" is basically defined as "a person who extends credit more than five times in a preceding calendar year or in a current calendar year for a transaction secured by a dwelling (Reg. Z, Section 226.2(a)(I))." An "arranger of credit" would include real estate brokers who arrange for sellers to take secondary loans.

CHAPTER 6
DISCRIMINATORY PRACTICES

In General

In evaluating the credit worthiness of mortgage loan applicants, lenders have traditionally engaged in practices that could be considered discriminatory against certain borrowers. For example, a working wife's income was usually not given as much weight as the husband's income because of the fear that the wife would stop working. Single women were sometimes required to have additional cosigners to their notes where single males would not be so required. These are clear examples of gender discrimination.

Federal law prohibits discrimination in the provision of credit, including mortgage loans, on the basis of race, color, national origin, religion, sex, marital status, age, receipt of public assistance funds, familial status, or the exercise of rights under the consumer credit protection laws. These rights are guaranteed under the Fair Housing Act (FHA) and the Equal Opportunity Act (ECOA), as more fully discussed below.

The Equal Credit Opportunity Act (ECOA)

Such discriminatory practices were made illegal by the Equal Credit Opportunity Act (ECOA) and Federal Reserve Regulation B, the regulation which interprets the ECOA. Initially, when this legislation went into effect in 1975, it prohibited the use of sex or marital status as factors in credit-granting decisions. Since 1977, when the Act was amended, seven other factors were outlawed as causes for discrimination in lending.

Thus, there are nine illegal factors which may not be used in the decision to grant credit, including: (i) sex; (ii) marital status; (iii) race, (iv) color, (v) religion, (vi) country of origin, (vii) age, (viii) receipt of public assistance benefits, and (ix) the good faith exercise of rights held under the Consumer Credit Protection Act. These prohibitions, which apply to all mortgage lenders, are sometimes called the "nifty nine."

In short, the ECOA is an attempt to assure that credit granting decisions are based solely on business judgment and repayment capacity. Indeed, a few states and regulators have added additional prohibitions against discriminating against the handicapped and others based upon their sexual orientation.

The ECOA requires lenders to notify the credit applicant of the decision made on their application. In the case of a credit denial, applicants must be notified of the reasons the credit was denied. The explanation must be in writing and made in within 30 days if "adverse action" is taken on a credit application. Offering different terms or a lesser amount is not considered adverse action, but rather is interpreted as a counter offer. In addition, action taken as a result of a borrower's default is not considered adverse action.

The notice required under the ECOA must contain a statement that discrimination is illegal, and include the list of factors considered discriminatory. The notice must also include the name of the federal agency responsible for enforcing the ECOA, which may vary, depending on the type of lender involved.

Credit is often denied for a combination of factors rather than for one specific factor. In the past, some creditors used a scoresheet containing certain factors, and denied credit when a certain aggregate score was not obtained. Under the ECOA, failure to attain the required score is not a sufficient reason in and of itself for denying credit. Rather, the specific reasons must be listed.

Redlining

Redlining is the practice by lending institutions of refusing to grant home mortgages or home-improvement loans for properties in certain designated urban neighborhoods. Redlining may consist of more subtle practices than a blunt refusal to lend in those designated areas. Such practices might include:

(1) requiring higher down payments and earlier loan-maturity dates;

(2) charging higher interest rates or special discount points for mortgages in redlined areas;

(3) establishing "minimum loan amounts" that exclude lower-priced, older urban housing; or

(4) underappraising properties in redlined areas.

Whether redlining actually exists is a hotly debated topic. Some studies have used deed records to indicate that commercial banks, mutual savings banks and savings and loan associations have put more of their money into suburbs than into the central cities. Other studies conclude that redlining is largely a myth. They contend that the relative small number of loans in the central or inner city is more a product of lower demand there, in response to general urban decay. Some even claim that central or inner-city borrowers receive preferential treatment because of the greater risk and cost of administration of loans in those areas.

The question of how to evaluate risk is at the heart of the redlining controversy. Community groups opposing redlining practices feel that mortgage lenders are discriminating against older urban properties and the people who live in those neighborhoods. They contend that redlining is a self-fulfilling prophecy. If lenders deny mortgage funds to an area because they feel it is declining, then the neighborhood will decline because home-owners cannot improve their properties and prospective homeowners cannot finance their purchases.

Many financial institutions take an opposite view. They point out that they have the responsibility to invest funds in a sound and prudent manner, and that this requirement dictates that they follow sound business practices in evaluating risk. In fact, many contend that they are now subsidizing inner-city neighborhoods by making loans on properties with greater potential for loss at terms similar to those found in the suburbs.

Opponents charge that redlining is a direct cause of and principal contributor to urban decline, and they seek additional legislation to force financial institutions to make more loans in older urban neighborhoods. They argue that the increased flow of funds would revitalize the inner-city and halt urban decay.

The financial institutions and their supporters assert that redlining is an effect and not a cause. Neighborhoods first deteriorate thus lenders are then more cautious about making loans in those areas. Their policy prescription is for the community to examine the real causes of urban decay and to establish programs and strategies to deal with those problems. If this is done, they contend, the mortgage funds will definitely follow.

The Home Disclosure Act

The Home Mortgage Disclosure Act (HMDA) is an attempt to eliminate the practice of "redlining" or refusing to make loans in certain geographical areas. It requires certain lenders to disclose the magnitude of mortgage loans made in each census tract or zip code area in the Standard Metropolitan Statistical Area (SMSA) that they serve.

The HMDA applies to lending institutions whose net worth exceeds $10 million and who make "federally related mortgages." With respect to the latter, the HDMA applies to any lender who is federally insured or regulated. In this way, the HMDA reporting requirements may serve to encourage lenders to make loans in all areas.

Community Reinvestment Act of 1977

The Community Reinvestment Act of 1977 specifically prohibits discrimination in lending on the basis of the age of the dwelling or its neighborhood. The Act also requires lending institutions to keep records on applicant characteristics such as race, sex, age and neighborhood, and to make them available for inspection. Racially discriminatory lending practices are also prohibited by the Fair Housing Act of 1968.

The "Effects Test"

In determining whether illegal discrimination has occurred, the Courts generally use what was first termed an "effects test" in *Griggs v. Duke Power Company*, 401 U.S. 424 (1971). The *Griggs* case appears to eliminate the requirement of proving "intent" to find that there has been discrimination. Thereafter, in a Senate Report issued in 1976, Congress specifically directed the judiciary to follow the reasoning in *Griggs*.

A companion case included in the Congressional directive, *Albermarle Paper Company v. Moody*, 422 U.S. 405 (1977), further suggested that showing a disproportionate racial impact created a "prima facie" discrimination case and shifted the burden of proof to the defendant to prove nondiscrimination.

In any event, the "effects test" has been undergoing continual judicial interpretation, which may have some impact on the way the ECOA is applied.

The Fair Credit Reporting Act

The Fair Credit Reporting Act (FCRA) is designed to help a person determine whether he has a good or bad credit rating. The FCRA primarily applies to credit bureaus. Before its passage, it was not possible to learn of the source of one's bad credit rating, much less be in a position to have it corrected. The FCRA is important to the real estate industry because lending decisions are often based on credit ratings.

In addition, real estate lenders may be considered "credit reporting agencies," and thereby be subject to the Act, if they give opinions in addition to factual information about the applicant's credit-worthiness.

If real estate lenders use information from a "consumer reporting agency" to deny credit or to increase one's interest rates, they must disclose to the prospective borrower the nature of the information and the name of the agency from which it was obtained. A provision exists for the consumer to have corrected any false, unsubstantiated or out-of-date facts adversely affecting their credit rating.

State Banking Agencies

Consumers who believe they have suffered illegal discrimination by a bank may also make a complaint to the appropriate governing agency. All states have banking agencies that regulate and supervise state-chartered banks. Many of them handle or refer problems and complaints about other types of financial institutions as well. Some also answer general questions about banking and consumer credit. When dealing with a federally chartered bank, the consumer is advised to check with the appropriate Federal Banking Agency.

A Directory of State Banking Agencies is set forth at Appendix 7.

CHAPTER 7
FORECLOSURE

In General

The term foreclosure generally refers to the legal process by which a mortgaged property may be sold to pay off a mortgage loan that is in default. If the borrower defaults on the mortgage payments, the lender has the right to foreclose on the property and sell it. The proceeds of the foreclosure sale are applied against the debt.

Mortgages made after the first mortgage are considered subordinate mortgages. The holder of a subordinate mortgage must wait until the first mortgagee is paid before recovering the debt owed on the subordinate mortgage. This is a precarious position to be in because if the sale does not result in enough money to cover both mortgages, the subordinate mortgagee is not paid in full, if at all.

If there is still an amount owing after the sale, the lender and any subordinate mortgagees have the right to seek a deficiency judgment against the borrower for any additional amounts owed. Alternatively, if the sale yields a profit, any amounts received above the outstanding debts are returned to the borrower.

Right of Acceleration

When a mortgage loan goes into default, the mortgagee usually has the right to "accelerate" the mortgage—i.e., to accelerate the maturity date of the note and render the entire debt due and payable. The acceleration clause is recognized as valid in all states and is also permitted in connection with government insured real estate loans. The typical acceleration clause is exercisable at the option of the holder of the note.

The reason almost all mortgage notes contain an acceleration clause is that in their absence, the mortgagee does not have a powerful remedy upon the mortgagor's default. Without an acceleration clause, the mortgagee's only possible means of recourse for default would be a suit to collect the amount of payments missed or a partial foreclosure for the amount of the mortgagor's default. The mortgagee would thereby be required to bring suit each time there was a default and would not be permitted to have one dispositive and final suit.

The acceleration clause permits the mortgagee to initiate only one lawsuit to collect the entire debt rather than being forced to sue in separate lawsuits for the amount due under each successive delinquent mortgage payment. The mortgagee can then proceed with foreclosure on the mortgage.

The interest increase provision of the acceleration clause allows the interest being paid on the debt to increase to either the maximum amount permitted by law or some other amount established in the clause when the mortgagor has defaulted on the loan payments. A sample provision is set forth below.

> Should default occur and acceleration of the full amount of the entire indebtedness is called for, interest on the entire amount of the indebtedness shall accrue thereafter at the maximum rate of interest then permitted under the laws of the State of [state name], or continue at the rate provided herein, whichever of said rates is greater.

Judicial Foreclosure

Foreclosure proceedings under a regular mortgage require judicial due process, similar to any breach of contract. Therefore, all of the procedures and defenses of any proceeding in litigation must be followed, which can be time-consuming and costly. The signatory mortgagors are necessary parties, as well as the lender. Everyone must be served with notice of the pending litigation as provided by state law for all judicial proceedings.

Upon final judgment, the court will order a public foreclosure sale. There is seldom any competitive bidding, particularly if the mortgagor has a right of redemption, because the real estate purchased does not usually lend itself to quick, speculative profits.

After the sale has taken place, the mortgagor's interest and all those interests acquired after the date of the initial recording of the mortgage are extinguished. When the sale price is accepted and confirmed by the court, a deed is issued. Although variations exist in state laws, it is usually difficult to have the sale set aside once the deed has been issued.

All foreclosure judgments may be collaterally attacked or appealed. When coupled with the statutory redemption rights existing in many states, the foreclosure procedures can be quite complicated and lengthy. Statutory redemption rights generally set out specific time periods following the foreclosure sale during which the mortgagor can "redeem" the real estate by reimbursing the foreclosure sale purchaser for all expenses.

Foreclosure Under a Deed of Trust

The foreclosure provision in a deed of trust is important. Typically, it provides that upon default, the beneficiary may request that the trustee sell the property at a foreclosure sale. There is usually a provision requiring notification to the mortgagor/owner of the impending sale.

Under a deed of trust, there is generally no requirement for a judicial proceeding. The foreclosure sale procedure is usually set out in the power of sale clause and is enforced as a contractual agreement between the parties. Thus, a deed of trust foreclosure sale is less expensive and less time-consuming than a judicial foreclosure sale.

Any party can bid at the foreclosure sale, although the mortgagee is typically the only bidder. When the nonjudicial foreclosure sale is properly conducted, it has the same effect as a judicial foreclosure. As a result, all persons claiming an interest under or through the mortgagor lose their interest when the foreclosure sale is completed. Title acquired by a foreclosure sale relates back to the date the deed of trust was recorded, extinguishing all subsequent liens and ownership interests, subject to the various rights of redemption.

Since the foreclosure sale under a deed of trust is usually a nonjudicial proceeding, the mortgagor cannot appeal it directly. On the other hand, he can initiate a lawsuit to enjoin the sale prior to its taking place, or to set aside the sale after it has taken place upon proof of irregularities e.g., violations of the mortgagor's contractual rights.

Nevertheless, if the mortgagor was properly notified and the foreclosure sale was properly executed, it will rarely be set aside. While this may seem somewhat harsh to the mortgagor, he still may be able to regain title under the statutory right of redemption existing in some states.

Deficiency Judgment

The foreclosure sale proceeds are used to pay off the mortgage debt. However, the mortgagee is never entitled to more money than the principal and interest due, plus expenses. If the foreclosure sale proceeds exceed the sum of the existing mortgage debt and the foreclosure sale expenses, the surplus, if any, goes to any subordinate lien-holders, and finally the mortgagor.

In most states, if the sale does not yield enough to cover the mortgagor's indebtedness, the mortgagee and any subordinate lienholder may obtain a "deficiency judgment" against the mortgagor. This means that the mortgagor still has the legal obligation to pay the unpaid balance of the loan.

However, as a practical matter, this debt may be difficult to collect, since the mortgagees have lost their security—i.e. the real estate sold at foreclosure—and no longer have a "lien" on any of the mortgagor's specific assets. This places the mortgagees in a similar position to the mortgagor's other "general" or "unsecured" creditors.

Equity of Redemption and Statutory Redemption

As discussed in Chapter 1, at one time in history, any failure to timely make a mortgage payment automatically caused the mortgagor to lose his entire interest in the land. Because of the severity of this provision, the law gradually moved toward other approaches that were less financially devastating to borrowers. These solutions included an equitable redemption and a statutory redemption for the mortgagor.

Equitable Redemption

The equitable redemption is available in all states to prevent foreclosure. It permits a mortgagor to prevent foreclosure from occurring by paying the mortgagee the principal and interest due, plus any expenses the mortgagee has incurred in attempting to collect the debt, and in initiating foreclosure proceedings. Equitable redemption may be exercised by mortgagors, junior mortgagees, the mortgagor's heir and devisees, any other party potentially adversely affected by foreclosure, and by anyone who buys the equity of redemption— i.e., "the right to redeem"— from the mortgagor.

Most courts have generally ruled that an equitable right of redemption may not be waived, and that waiver clauses in a mortgage are null and void, although this is not always the case. Legally, these courts hold that an equitable right of redemption is automatically a part of every mortgage and cannot be contractually modified by the parties. To decide otherwise would be unfair to mortgagors, as some lenders might otherwise refuse to lend unless the equity of redemption was waived.

Statutory Redemption

Statutory redemption rights generally permit a mortgagor to redeem mortgaged property after the foreclosure sale. Not all states permit statutory redemption, and in those that do permit it, the maximum permissible redemption time period varies from approximately six months to two years.

The reader is advised to check the law of his or her own jurisdiction to determine the availability of statutory redemption.

Priority of Liens

Where more than one mortgage exists on the same property, questions of priority are significant when it comes to a foreclosure sale. One of the basic functions of foreclosure is to put the foreclosure sale purchaser in the shoes of the mortgagor at the time he executed the mortgage being foreclosed. As a result, the purchaser will obtain a title that is free and clear of all mortgages or other liens junior or subordinate to the mortgage being foreclosed.

Thus, a sale purchaser will generally get title free of the second mortgage. This means that any junior liens are wiped out. If, however, the sale brings more than the first mortgage debt, the second mortgagee should normally have a claim to the surplus that is superior to that of the mortgagor.

Because the foreclosure sale generally extinguishes all inferior lien interests, the holders of inferior liens often bid on or buy property at foreclosure sales to make sure the sale price is sufficient to cover the outstanding loan balance owed them. Also, as previously discussed, inferior lien holders may exercise the equity of redemption to protect their lien interest.

If it is the second mortgage that is in default instead of the first mortgage, the second mortgagee forecloses. In this case as well, the sale should put the purchaser in the shoes of the mortgagor as of the time the mortgage being foreclosed was executed. As a result, a purchaser will obtain a fee title subject to the first mortgage because the foreclosure of a junior mortgage normally does not affect the status of a senior mortgage on the property. The property is sold "subject to" the superior security interest(s). The purchaser must make payments on the prior existing indebtedness, and is considered to be "subrogated," or placed in the position of the original mortgagor on the inferior lien.

Thus, in the foreclosure process the purchaser at a foreclosure sale is said to have acquired the right to "redeem up," and the trustee or court "forecloses down." This simply means that foreclosure dissolves all inferior interests, and the foreclosure sale purchaser acquires the right to pay off the superior interests.

Lien priorities generally follow the so-called "barber-shop rule," meaning that the first in time gets priority. Priority is established by compliance with recording acts, so (i) the lack of knowledge of previous mortgages, and (ii) the date that competing mortgages are recorded, are both important factors in determining priority of mortgage payment in case of foreclosure.

Thus, in calculating what a purchaser should bid at a foreclosure sale, he or she should at least subtract the amount of the first mortgage, free and clear of liens, from the market value of the property. Although the sale purchaser is generally not personally liable on the first mortgage debt, he or she runs the risk that the first mortgage will be foreclosed and that he will lose his title to the property if he does not satisfy it.

CHAPTER 8
THE REAL ESTATE SETTLEMENT
PROCEDURES ACT

In General

The Real Estate Settlement Procedures Act (RESPA) is a federal disclosure statute enacted to help consumers become better shoppers for settlement services. RESPA requires that borrowers receive disclosures at various times. Some disclosures spell out the costs associated with the settlement, outline lender servicing and escrow account practices and describe business relationships between settlement service providers.

The Act was also designed to eliminate kickbacks and unearned fees. Congress concluded in the Real Estate Settlement Procedures Act of 1974 that consumers need protection from ". . . unnecessarily high settlement charges caused by certain abusive practices that have developed in some areas of the country."

Applicability

RESPA relates to all federally related mortgage loans. In order to be covered under RESPA, a mortgage loan must meet the following three criteria: (1) the loan must be for the purchase of a one to four family residential dwelling; (2) the loan must constitute a first lien on the property; and (3) the loan must be made by or for a lender supervised by a federal agency. In practice, the majority of residential real estate loans are subject to the Act.

Under the Act, when a lender receives an application for a federally related mortgage loan, the lender is required to provide the prospective borrower with: (1) information concerning settlement costs which are contained in a booklet published by the United States Department of Housing and Urban Development (HUD); and (2) a "good faith estimate" of all charges to be paid at the closing of the loan.

Good Faith Estimate

RESPA requires that, when one applies for a loan, the lender or mortgage broker must give the applicant a Good Faith Estimate of settlement service charges he or she will likely have to pay on or before closing. If the applicant does not get this Good Faith Estimate at the time they apply, the lender or mortgage broker is required to mail or deliver it to the applicant within the next three business days.

It should be noted that the amounts listed on the Good Faith Estimate are only estimates. Actual costs may vary and changing market conditions can affect prices. The lender's estimate is not a guarantee. The applicant should keep the Good Faith Estimate so that they can compare it with the final settlement costs.

A sample Good Faith Estimate is set forth at Appendix 8.

Loan Servicing Transfers

Under the Act, the lender is further required to disclose to the loan applicant, in writing, whether their mortgage loan payments may be transferred to another party, and the likelihood that such an event will occur. This is known as a "servicing transfer," under which the collection of principal, interest and escrow account payments are transferred to another party. This disclosure must be made at the time of application or within the next three business days, whether or not the lender expects that someone else will be servicing the loan.

A copy of the RESPA Servicing Disclosure is set forth at Appendix 9.

Settlement Statement (HUD-1)

In addition, at or before the closing, the lender is required to provide both the borrower and the seller with a completed Uniform Settlement Statement Form, commonly referred to as a "HUD-1" Form, which includes the exact amounts of all of the closing costs.

The borrower has the right to inspect the HUD-1 Settlement Statement. This statement itemizes the services provided and the fees charged. This form is filled out by the settlement agent who will conduct the settlement. The fully completed HUD-1 Settlement Statement generally must be delivered or mailed to the borrower at or before the settlement. In cases where there is no settlement meeting, the escrow agent will mail the HUD-1 after settlement.

A sample HUD-1 Form is set forth at Appendix 10.

Affiliated Businesses and Illegal Referrals

The law also prohibits anyone from giving or taking a fee, kickback, or anything of value under an agreement that business will be referred to a specific person or organization. For example, sometimes, several businesses that offer settlement services are owned or controlled by a common corporate parent. These businesses are known as "affiliates." When a lender, real estate broker, or other participant in your settlement refers you to an affiliate for a settlement service, RESPA requires the referring party to give you an Affiliated Business Arrangement Disclosure. This form will remind you that you are generally not required, with certain exceptions, to use the affiliate and are free to shop for other providers.

It is illegal under RESPA for anyone to pay or receive a fee, kickback or anything of value because they agree to refer settlement service business to a particular person or organization. For example, your mortgage lender may not pay your real estate broker $250 for referring you to the lender. It is also illegal for anyone to accept a fee or part of a fee for services if that person has not actually performed settlement services for the fee. For example, a lender may not add to a third party's fee, such as an appraisal fee, and keep the difference.

Nevertheless, RESPA does not prevent title companies, mortgage brokers, appraisers, attorneys, settlement/closing agents and others, who actually perform a service in connection with the mortgage loan or the settlement, from being paid for the reasonable value of their work.

The law is primarily aimed at eliminating arrangements whereby one party agrees to return part of their fee in order to obtain business from a referring party. One of the negative results of such an arrangement is that fees are unnecessarily raised to cover the hidden "referral fee," thus harming the prospective borrower.

There are criminal penalties which include both fines and imprisonment for violations of the law. There are also provisions whereby the victim of such an arrangement may recover three times the amount of the kickback, rebate, or referral fee involved, through a private lawsuit. In addition, if the action is successful, the court may award attorney's fees and costs.

CHAPTER 9
THE REAL ESTATE
LOAN PROCESS

The Accepted Offer

The process of purchasing a home and obtaining financing for that purchase begins when the buyer makes an offer on the property, and the seller accepts the offer. Following acceptance of the offer, a memorandum of agreement is usually prepared, which sets forth the basic details of the transaction, and identifies the brokers, the parties, and their respective attorneys.

In some jurisdictions, a binder—payment of a small sum of money which evidences the buyer's good faith—is made. However, the legal enforceability of the binder as a contract is questionable, thus, it should not be depended upon in order to secure the deal.

The Real Estate Contract

The next step in the real estate transaction involves drafting the real estate contract, which is generally done by the seller's attorney. The contracts are then sent to the buyer's attorney for review and signature, and returned to the seller's attorney with the buyer's downpayment, which is held in escrow until closing.

The real estate contract, to be valid, must contain all of the essential terms of a legal contract, including an offer; acceptance of the offer; and consideration, i.e., an exchange of something of value by each of the parties. Further, the parties to the contract must be legally competent, must have voluntarily entered into the contract, and the contract must be for a legal purpose which is possible to perform.

The contract must also comply with the statute of frauds. The statute of frauds is a legal doctrine which provides, in part, that all contracts for the sale and purchase of real estate are required to be in writing. Further, the writing must be signed by the parties.

Although property can be legally conveyed without a real estate contract, it is the contract that creates the legal obligation between the parties to perform as agreed. For example, without the contract, one of the parties could simply renege on the deal, and the other party would not have any legal recourse. The contract provides specific remedies in case one of the parties defaults, such as forfeiture of the downpayment to the seller, or money damages to the buyer.

Because land is considered unique, and money damages may not be a sufficient remedy to the buyer, the doctrine of specific performance may apply. If the buyer sues for specific performance—i.e. to force the seller to perform under the contract—the judge may compel the seller to turn the property over to the buyer as agreed.

The contract also sets forth the financing contingencies of the buyer, which basically permit the buyer to get out of the contract if he or she is unable to secure the type of financing set forth in the contract.

For example, the contract may specify a mortgage contingency of 90% financing of the purchase price. If the buyer is unable to qualify for a loan on those terms, but the lender agrees to finance 80%, the buyer has the option of going forward with the lesser financing, or of invoking the mortgage contingency clause to get out of the contract without losing the downpayment.

However, if the buyer qualifies for the 90% loan, he or she must go forward with the purchase, or risk forfeiting the downpayment to the seller for damages.

The contract may also provide remedies if a physical inspection of the property reveals any problems, such as termite infestation or structural damage. Such remedies may include a purchase price reduction, or a requirement that the necessary repairs be made as a condition to closing.

Selecting a Lender

Although a prospective homebuyer may purchase a home on an all cash basis, it is more likely that the buyer will obtain a mortgage to finance a large part of the purchase price through a real estate lender. As set forth below, the most common real estate lenders are banks and mortgage companies.

Prior to selecting a lender, the reader is advised to check the real estate or business sections in the newspaper for information on current interest rates, and to undertake some comparative shopping. One should call several lenders for rates and terms based on the type of mortgage sought.

For example, if the buyer is looking for an adjustable rate mortgage (ARM), as discussed in Chapter 4, it is important to inquire about the maximum interest rate that can be charged during the life of the loan, how often the rate can change, and the index used to determine the rate change.

It is also important to ask each lender for a complete list of closing costs and inquire as to which costs will be refunded to you if the loan application is not approved.

A Closing Cost Estimator is set forth at Appendix 11.

Sources of Real Estate Financing

Some companies, known as "mortgage brokers," will find a homebuyer a mortgage lender who is willing to finance the buyer's purchase. A mortgage broker may operate as an independent business and may not be operating as your "agent" or representative. Your mortgage broker may be paid by the lender, the borrower, or both. It is important to inquire as to the fees the mortgage broker will receive for its services, which is generally paid at closing.

Most home mortgage loans are made by savings and loan associations, commercial banks, mortgage bankers, credit unions, or building and loan associations. However, anyone, including a private individual, may make a mortgage loan.

The Mortgage Application

Once the prospective borrower has selected the lender with whom he or she wishes to apply, the first step is to complete the loan application.

A sample Uniform Residential Loan Application is set forth at Appendix 12.

In order to process the loan application, the loan officer will generally require a copy of the memorandum of agreement or real estate contract. The loan officer may also request a personal financial statement and a request for verification of the applicant's employment and banking information. In general, the applicant will be required to pay a loan application fee which may cover, among other things, the cost of an appraisal of the property, and the lender's cost in obtaining a copy of the applicant's credit report.

In reviewing the loan application, the lender will consider a number of factors in deciding whether to approve the loan. The most important criteria are the credit worthiness of the applicant and the applicant's financial ability to make the loan payments.

For example, the lender will review the applicant's past record of loan repayment, net worth and current earning capacity. This information is obtained partly from the financial statement prepared by the applicant, and partly from other sources such as credit bureaus, independent credit references, and sources provided or suggested by the applicant.

In determining whether the applicant is financially able to make the loan payments, the lender will consider the applicant's housing expense ratio. The two elements which make up a housing expense ratio are (i) the monthly out-of-pocket costs for continued ownership of a home; and (ii) the monthly income generated by the prospective borrower. Many lenders require that the monthly housing payment be no greater than 25% to 35% of the borrower's monthly income.

The lender will also carefully review the appraisal report to determine the value of the property. The appraised value of the property generally determines how much the lender will be willing to finance. Most conventional lenders will finance up to 80% of the appraised value of the property.

A sample Uniform Residential Appraisal Report is set forth at Appendix 13.

Under federal law, lenders are required to notify credit applicants of the action taken on their loan application within thirty days. If the application is denied, the lender must inform the applicant of the reasons for the rejection.

Lock-In Rates

"Locking in" one's rate or points at the time of application or during the processing of the loan will keep the rate and/or points from changing until settlement or closing of the escrow process. The prospective borrower should ask the lender if they charge a fee to lock-in the rate and, if so, whether the fee reduces the amount one must pay for points. In addition, it is important to find out how long the "lock-in" rate is effective, what happens if it expires, and whether the lock-in fee is refundable if the loan application is rejected.

Loan Commitment

A loan commitment is a promise by a lender to make a loan at some future date. The loan commitment's terms and conditions for a single family residential purchaser might be as brief as those contained in the following letter:

Dear Borrower:

We hereby commit to make you a mortgage loan on the property located at [address of property]. Said loan shall be in the amount of [$ amount of loan] amortized over a term of [#] years at an interest rate of [xx%] percent, subject to the terms of the interest adjustment provision in the mortgage note, and shall be closed on our Association's documents and governed by the provisions contained therein.

This commitment is also granted subject to satisfactory evidence of title and other related items required for the closing of this transaction and there being no substantial change in the collateral or in your credit status.

This commitment will expire if: (a) the loan to be granted under the terms of this commitment is not closed for any reason whatsoever, within [#] days of the date of this letter, or (b) the loan to be granted under this commitment is closed whereby the terms and conditions of the mortgage and the mortgage note will supersede this commitment.

Thank you for the opportunity of permitting us to be of service to you.

Signed, Lender.

Generally, a lender who does not provide a loan as promised in their commitment letter will be required to pay damages to the borrower to the extent of (1) the difference between the interest at the contract rate and the rate of interest the borrower must pay on the open market; (2) any of the costs of obtaining new financing; and (3) any other consequential damages contemplated by the parties at the time of the loan commitment.

In connection with the commitment letter, the lender usually requires the borrower to pay a "commitment fee." The commitment fee is supposed to compensate the lender for the administrative costs of underwriting the loan and holding the funds available for the borrower's use. If the borrower pays a commitment fee which is termed non-refundable, and the borrower obtains financing elsewhere, it has been held that the lender is entitled to keep the commitment fee as damages for breach of contract or compensation for holding the loan money for the borrower.

CHAPTER 10
THE REAL ESTATE CLOSING

In General

The real estate "closing" is the finalization of the real estate transaction which takes place soon after the mortgage has been approved. The closing is usually held at the office of the attorney for one of the participants, e.g., the buyer, seller or lender.

At the closing, each of the parties finalizes their part of the agreement. The Buyer pays the purchase price of the property to the Seller, less any deposits already made. There are also adjustments based on items such as property taxes and utility bills incurred during the time the Seller held title to the property, which may have been paid by the Seller, or which are payable by the Seller. If the Buyer is financing part of the purchase price, the Lender will pay the loan proceeds to the Seller on the Buyer's behalf.

Closing Costs

"Closing Costs" are those additional costs the Buyer or Seller must pay in connection with closing the real estate transaction. Common closing costs include the following:

Title Insurance

Title insurance is an insurance policy which protects the lender and buyer against loss due to disputes over ownership of a property which may arise after the real estate transaction closes. In some states, attorneys offer title insurance as part of their services in examining title and providing a title opinion. The attorney's fee may include the title insurance premium. In other states, a title insurance company or title agent directly provides the title insurance.

In order to insure the title, prior to the closing, the title examiner undertakes an investigation of municipal records to ensure that the seller is the legal owner of a property and can convey marketable title. This examination is known as a "title search." The title search also reveals any liens or encumbrances that may exist against the property, which must be satisfied at or before closing.

Lenders or title insurance agents often also require a survey to mark the boundaries of the property. A survey is a drawing of the property showing the perimeter boundaries and marking the location of the house and other improvements. The buyer may be able to avoid the cost of a complete survey if they can locate the person who previously surveyed the property and request that the survey be updated.

Prior to the settlement or closing of the escrow, the title insurance company will issue a "Commitment to Insure" or preliminary report or "binder" containing a summary of any defects in title which have been identified by the title search, as well as any exceptions from the title insurance policy's coverage. The commitment is usually sent to the lender for use until the title insurance policy is issued at or after the closing. The buyer can request a copy of the commitment, or have a copy sent to their attorney, so that they can object if there are matters affecting the title which the buyer did not agree to accept when he or she signed the agreement of sale.

If the buyer is financing the purchase, the lender will require that, at the very least, the lender's interest in the property—to the extent of the amount of the mortgage—is covered by title insurance. Nevertheless, a lender's title insurance policy does not protect the buyer. Similarly, the prior owner's policy does not protect the new buyer.

If the buyer wants to be protected from claims by others against the new home, they will need an "owner's policy." When a claim does occur, it can be financially devastating to an owner who is uninsured. If you buy an owner's policy, it is usually much less expensive if you buy it at the same time and with the same insurer as the lender's policy.

The buyer also has the option to pay an additional premium to cover the difference between the mortgage amount and the purchase price. It is also wise to purchase—for a small additional fee—a market value rider. A market value rider provides that the property is covered up to the fair market value at the time the claim is made.

For example, if the purchase price of the property is $50,000, and the mortgage amount is $40,000, the lender will require that a title insurance policy is purchased indemnifying the lender up to $40,000. The buyer may pay an additional premium to have the property covered for the full purchase price of $50,000. However, if a claim is made ten years after the purchase, when the fair market value of the property is $200,000, the insured is only covered up to $50,000. Purchase of the market value rider would indemnify the insured up to the full market value at the time of the loss, which in this case is $200,000.

Under RESPA, the seller may not require the buyer, as a condition of the sale, to purchase title insurance from any particular title company. Generally, the lender will require title insurance from a company that is acceptable to it. A violation of this provision makes the seller liable in an amount equal to three times all charges associated with the title insurance.

In most cases the buyer can shop for and choose a company that meets the lender's standards. One may also compare rates among various title insurance companies. If the property being purchased has changed hands within the last several years, the title company may offer a "reissue rate," which may be less costly. The buyer should inquire as to what services and limitations on coverage are provided under each policy so that they can decide whether coverage purchased at a higher rate may be better for their needs.

Nevertheless, in many states, title insurance premium rates are established by the state and may not be negotiable. The reader is advised to check the law of his or her jurisdiction in this regard.

Escrow Account for Homeowner's Insurance and Real Estate Tax Payments

The borrower will generally have to contribute funds into an escrow account at closing for payment of homeowner insurance premiums and real estate tax payments. The lender generally collects 3 to 6 month's of payments at closing.

The escrow account is an account held by the lender to which the borrower pays monthly installments, collected as part of the monthly mortgage payment, for homeowner insurance premiums and real estate tax payments. The lender disburses escrow account funds on behalf of the borrower when payments become due.

At the settlement or within the next 45 days, the person servicing the loan must give the borrower an initial escrow account statement. That form will show all of the payments which are expected to be deposited into the escrow account and all of the disbursements which are expected to be made from the escrow account during the year ahead. The lender or servicer will review the escrow account annually and send the borrower a disclosure each year which shows the prior year's activity and any adjustments necessary in the escrow payments that will be made in the forthcoming year.

Escrow accounts are widely used to protect mortgagees, as further set forth below.

Homeowner's Insurance

Both mortgagor and mortgagee have insurable interests regarding the mortgaged premises. The insurable interest of the mortgagor is the value of the mortgaged premises and the mortgagee's interest is the amount of the mortgage debt. Neither party normally would have an interest in the proceeds of the other's policy, since courts traditionally have looked upon insurance as a purely personal contract of indemnity. On the other hand, a mortgagee is not allowed to collect both the proceeds of its own policy and the debt because the insurer becomes subrogated to the mortgage debt.

The normal practice today is for the mortgagee to require that the mortgagor carry casualty insurance insuring the interests of both parties. Two types of such policy provisions are the open mortgage clause—known as the loss payable policy—and the standard mortgage clause.

Under a loss payable policy, the policy is issued to the mortgagor with a clause providing that the loss be payable to the mortgagor and to the mortgagee as its interest may appear.

The standard mortgage clause is more commonly used today and generally provides as follows:

> Loss or damage, if any, under this policy shall be payable to the mortgagee as his interest may appear, and this insurance, as to the mortgagee only therein, shall not be invalidated by any act or neglect of the mortgagor or owner of the within described property, nor by any change in the title or ownership of the property, nor by the occupation of the premises for purposes more hazardous than are permitted by this policy, provided, that in case the mortgagor or owner shall neglect to pay any premium under this policy, the mortgagee shall on demand pay the same.

Most lenders will not lend money to buy a home in a flood hazard area unless the borrower pays for flood insurance. Some government loan programs will not allow a borrower to purchase a home that is located in a flood hazard area. The lender may charge a fee to check for flood hazards. The borrower should be notified if flood insurance is required. If a change in flood insurance maps brings the home within a flood hazard area after the loan is made, the lender or servicer may require the borrower to buy flood insurance at that time.

Real Estate Tax Payments

Mortgagees are adamant that the mortgagor promptly pay real estate taxes and special assessments. Mortgagees are understandably vigilant about this because if the tax on the land or special assessments for local improvements are not paid, both the mortgagee and mortgagor may lose their interests.

The state generally has the right to foreclose on property to collect back taxes. Further, the state's claim will override all prior interests. In other words, a "first" mortgage on real estate can be wiped out by a sale under a subsequently arising real estate tax lien. This is why mortgagees generally include mortgage clauses specifically imposing the duty to pay taxes on the mortgagor which make failure to do so a cause for acceleration of the mortgage debt.

The Loan Origination Fee

The loan origination fee—also known as "discount points"—is the service charge made by the lender for the granting of the loan. It is commonly referred to in terms of "points"—i.e., a percentage point of the loan amount. For example, on a $100,000 loan, a two-point loan origination fee would be two thousand dollars.

Private Mortgage Insurance

Private Mortgage Insurance (PMI) is an insurance policy that protects the lender in case the borrower defaults on the mortgage loan. PMI is generally not required with conventional loans if the down payment is at least 20%. If the equity in the property is less than 80%, the borrower will have to pay PMI premiums.

Private mortgage insurance enables the lender to make a loan which the lender considers a higher risk. The borrower may be billed monthly, annually, by an initial lump sum, or some combination of these practices for the mortgage insurance premium.

Mortgage insurance should not be confused with mortgage life, credit life or disability insurance, which are designed to pay off a mortgage in the event of the borrower's death or disability.

The borrower may also be offered "lender paid" mortgage insurance ("LPMI"). Under LPMI plans, the lender purchases the mortgage insurance and pays the premiums to the insurer. The lender will increase the interest rate to pay for the premiums—but LPMI may reduce the settlement costs.

The borrower cannot cancel LPMI or government mortgage insurance during the life of your loan. However, it may be possible to cancel private mortgage insurance at some point, such as when the borrower's equity in the property increases to 80%.

Prepaid Interest

Prepaid interest refers to interest on the real estate loan that is paid in advance of when it is due. Prepaid interest is typically charged to the borrower at closing to cover the interest on the loan between the closing date until the end of the month

Closing Documents

The legal documents which finalize the real estate transaction are executed at the closing. Of primary importance, as further discussed below, the mortgagor is required to sign the Mortgage and Promissory Note, among many other financing documents; and the seller is required to execute the Deed.

The Mortgage

The mortgage is a written instrument, duly executed by the Borrower at the real estate closing, and delivered to the Lender. The mortgage creates a lien upon the property being financed, as security for the payment of the real estate loan. The language in the mortgage document basically parallels that contained in the Mortgage Note, as more fully set forth below.

A sample Plain Language Mortgage is set forth at Appendix 14.

The Mortgage Note

The mortgage note—also known as a real estate lien note or promissory note depending on the jurisdiction—is the legal document that represents the mortgagor's actual "promise" to repay the loan at a specified interest rate over a stated time period.

The mortgagor is required to execute a mortgage note in addition to the mortgage because the mortgage note, unlike the mortgage, is considered a "negotiable instrument." Thus, the mortgage note, like a bank draft, can be endorsed on the back and sold to an investor. The mortgage is the document that evidences a lien interest against the real estate. Thus, both instruments serve entirely different functions, but are dependent on each other to (i) effect a sufficient promise to pay; and (ii) perfect a lien interest in real estate.

It is a very common practice in the mortgage business for mortgage companies to sell millions of dollars in loans using the mortgage note as the primary instrument of transfer. The purchaser of the mortgage note becomes a "holder in due course," which means he takes the note free and clear of all defenses that the maker may have, except for fraud in the inducement of the note, thus guaranteeing that all payments will be made on the note.

Legally, because a mortgage note is a negotiable instrument, It is considered to be an unconditional promise to pay by the maker of the note. Although a note holder may accept late payments, the general rule is that the holder of the note has the absolute right to accelerate all the payments—i.e., declare the total amount of the note due when a payment is late.

The note holder also has the right to foreclose under the deed of trust which secures the payment of that note. This is true even if the underlying mortgage was not assigned to the new note holder because the right to foreclose under the old mortgage also passes to the new note holder.

Every mortgage note will include the following provisions:

1. The mortgagor's promise to pay the mortgage.

2. The principal—i.e., the amount of the debt.

3. The interest rate charged on the outstanding principal.

4. The time and amount of principal and interest payments.

5. A reference to the note's security.

6. The mortgagor's signature.

The following clauses are not essential to the creation of the note but may be inserted for business reasons:

1. A provision that matured—i.e. overdue—principal and interest shall also earn interest at a specified rate.

2. The penalty charge for prepayment of the debt, if applicable. The mortgagee may seek a prepayment penalty to assure an acceptable rate of return on the loan.

3. Whether prepayments will be credited against the principal or against future interest or payments.

4. Default provisions, such as an acceleration clause. An acceleration clause permits the mortgagee to initiate only one lawsuit to collect the entire debt rather than being forced to sue in separate lawsuits for the amount due under each successive delinquent mortgage payment.

5. A requirement that the mortgagor pay the mortgagee's attorney fees necessitated by the mortgagor's default.

6. A provision waiving any legal requirement that a mortgagor must be given notice when each successive payment becomes due since this information is contained in the mortgagor's copy of the note.

A sample Mortgage Note is set forth at Appendix 15.

The Deed

The Deed is the most common method of transferring ownership in real estate. At the closing, the Deed is executed and turned over to the party who is responsible for its recording. This is usually the title examiner.

In order for the deed to be valid, it must meet certain requirements, as set forth below.

(1) The seller of the property, also known as the grantor, must have the legal right to transfer the property and must sign the deed over to the buyer. The grantor may be an individual, a partnership, a corporation, a governmental authority, or someone in a fiduciary capacity who has authority to transfer ownership of the property, such as a court order or a written and recorded agreement. Examples of fiduciaries are trustees, executors, and administrators.

(2) The buyer of the property, also known as the grantee, must be accurately identified, and the addresses for both the grantor and grantee must be stated.

(3) The deed must also specify the form of ownership which is being transferred, and the language of conveyance which expresses the intent to transfer the property.

(4) Another requirement for any valid contract, is the recital of consideration, i.e., the exchange of something of value by each party. In this case, consideration refers to the payment of a sum of money by the buyer, and the surrender of the deed to the property by the seller. The usual recital of consideration in a deed reads as follows:

> Witnesseth, that the party of the first part, in consideration of ten dollars and other valuable consideration paid by the party of the second part, does hereby grant and release unto the party of the second part . . . all that certain plot, piece or parcel of land . . .

The exact purchase price is generally not stated in the Deed for confidentiality reasons. The fact that there is a recital of consideration suffices to satisfy the requirement.

(5) The deed must be delivered to, and accepted by, the grantee. This is evidenced by the payment of the purchase price in exchange for the deed.

(6) The signatures on the deed must be acknowledged by a notary public in order for the deed to be accepted for recording.

(7) The deed must also contain a legal description of the property which is the subject of the transaction. The legal description is based on

a detailed survey of the property. It is important that the description be as accurate as possible so that the parties understand exactly what is being conveyed. There are three common types of legal descriptions used:

(a) Metes and Bounds—"Metes" refers to the actual measurement of the property, and "Bounds" refers to the physical boundaries of the property. The property description details the direction of, and the distance between, physical points of reference.

(b) Record Plat Descriptions—Record plat descriptions refers to the method of describing the property by lot and block, also incorporating the existing method of legal description into the detailed record plat.

(c) The Rectangular System—The rectangular system is the method used by the majority of states. The rectangular system uses a grid with lines running north and south—known as meridians—and lines running east and west—known as parallels. These lines create squares, each of which represents a certain distance within the town. The squares are divided and subdivided until the land within each section is identified.

The most common types of deeds used to convey property include:

(1) The Full Covenant and Warranty Deed—The full covenant and warranty deed is one in which the grantor fully warrants, or guarantees, that there is good title to the property. This guarantee dates back through the chain of title, and each prior grantor of a warranty deed may be liable to the buyer if a claim is made which is traced back to the date of conveyance by a particular prior grantor.

(2) The Bargain and Sale Deed With Covenant—The bargain and sale deed with covenant is the simplest and most commonly used deed. It conveys all of the rights and interests that the grantor of the property holds. It also contains a covenant warranting good title to the property. However, unlike the full covenant and warranty deed, the bargain and sale covenant only relates to claims arising out of the period of ownership of the grantor who is conveying the deed.

(3) The Bargain and Sale Deed Without Covenant—The bargain and sale deed without covenant does not contain the statement of warranty of title. It is similar to the quitclaim deed in that it does not protect the buyer from liens or other third party claims on the property should they arise. The difference between the quitclaim deed and the bargain and sale deed without covenant is that the latter contains language which, at the very least, implies that the grantor actually owns the property being conveyed.

(4) The Quitclaim Deed—The quitclaim deed, like the bargain and sale deed without covenant, conveys all of the rights and interest that the grantor of the property holds, however, it does not contain language which implies that the grantor actually owns the property. Thus, if the grantor has no rights to the property, the grantee, in reality, receives nothing by way of the deed.

(5) The Referee's Deed—The referee's deed is used to convey property by the referee following a foreclosure sale. Like the quitclaim deed, the referee's deed does not contain covenants warranting title.

(6) The Executor's Deed—The executor's deed is used by the executor of a will to convey property of a decedent's estate. The executor's deed usually contains a covenant against the executor's acts, similar to the covenant against grantor's acts contained in the bargain and sale deed.

Following the closing, the person responsible for recording the deed—usually the title company representative—files the deed, along with the required fee, with the appropriate authority. It is important that the deed be recorded as soon thereafter as practicable so as to give the public constructive notice of the transaction, and make the transfer part of the chain of title for that property. Because laws may vary, the reader is cautioned to check the recording requirements of their own jurisdiction to make sure that their rights are preserved.

Taking Possession

Following the closing, the buyers are generally entitled to take immediate possession of the house, unless some other arrangement has been made. If the seller is unable to immediately vacate the house, the contract usually provides for certain payments to be made to the buyers for each day the seller occupies the property after the closing. The contract usually requires the seller to turn over the property in a "broom-swept" condition. This generally means that the seller removes all personal property and debris from the premises.

APPENDICES

APPENDIX 1

FHA CLOSING REQUIREMENTS

FHA FORM NO. 1022
Rev. 4/66

U. S. DEPARTMENT OF HOUSING AND URBAN DEVELOPMENT
FEDERAL HOUSING ADMINISTRATION

FHA LEGAL REQUIREMENTS FOR CLOSING
Sections 207, 220, 221(d)(4), 231 and 232

Project Name: _____ Project No.: _____

Name of Mortgagor: _____ Address: _____

Name of Mortgagee: _____ Address: _____

The Closing Attorney will obtain three copies of all closing documents. These will be Originals ("Or"), Executed ("E"), Certified ("C") or Conformed ("Cn") as indicated below.

PART A. FOR INSURANCE OF ADVANCES

Instruments:		Copies
1. Assignment of Commitment, if any	E,	2 Cn
2. Regulation of Mortgagor:		
(a) Regulatory Agreement (2466) For 231-NP and 232-NP use 2466 e. For 232 use 2466 or 2466 e signed by Mortgagor and 2466 NHL signed by Lessee, if any.	E,	2 Cn
(b) Corporate Charter, Partnership Agreement, or other agreement establishing mortgagor (required provisions in instructions to 2466)	C,	2 Cn
3. Deferred Note, if any (2223)	3 Cn	
4. Lease (if mortgage is on leasehold)	C,	2 Cn
5. Land Disposition Contract and Deed, if any (Required only for projects in urban renewal areas)	E,	2 C
6. Title Policy	E,	2 Cn
7. Evidence of Zoning Compliance	3 Cn	
8. Building Permits	3 Cn	
9. Surveyor's Plat	3 Cn	
10. Surveyor's Certificate (2457)	Or,	2 Cn
11. Note (FHA Form for State)	3 Cn	
12. Mortgage (FHA Form for State)	3 Cn	
13. Building Loan Agreement (2441)	E,	2 Cn
14. Construction Contract, Lump Sum (2442) or Cost Plus (2442 A)	E,	2 Cn
15. Assurance of Completion:		
(a) Contract Bond Dual-Obligee (2452) or	E,	2 Cn
(b) Completion Assurance Agreement (2450)	E,	2 Cn
16. Owner-Architect Agreement (2719-A, or 2719-B, or 2719-C)	E,	2 Cn
17. Assurance of Completion of Off-Site Facilities:		
(a) Off-Site Bond (2479) or	E,	2 Cn
(b) Escrow Agreement for Off-Site Facilities (2446) with Schedule "A"	E,	2 Cn
18. Assurance of Utility Services (Water, Electricity, Sewer, Gas, Heat)	E,	2 Cn
19. Contractor's and/or Mortgagor's Cost Breakdown (2328)	Or,	2 Cn
20. Mortgagee's Certificate (2434)	Or,	2 Cn
21. Mortgagor's Certificate (2433)	Or,	2 Cn
22. Mortgagor's Oath (2478)	Or,	2 Cn
23. Mortgagor's Attorney's Opinion	Or,	2 Cn
* 24. Contractor's Certification (2482)	Or,	2 Cn
* 25. Agreement and Certification (3305 for 207) or	Or,	2 Cn
Agreement and Certification (3306 for 220 and 221 (d)(4))	Or,	2 Cn
26. Sponsor's Certification (3437) for 231-NP and 232-NP	Or,	2 Cn
27. Guaranty Agreement (3436) for 231-NP and 232-NP if subsidized	E,	2 Cn

* To have been filed with Director at least 30 days prior to initial closing.

- 2 -

PART B. FOR INSURANCE UPON COMPLETION

NOTE: In cases of Insurance upon Completion, the required closing documents will vary substantially from those in cases of Insurance of Advances. The required closing documents in cases of Insurance Upon Completion will be the following:

1 through 13 will be identical with 1 through 13 in cases of Insurance of Advances. The additional documents will be

14.	Construction Contract, if used	E,	2 Cn
15.	Guarantee Against Latent Defects (Bond [3259] or Escrow)	E,	2 Cn
16.	Escrow Deposit Agreement for Incomplete On-Site Improvements with Schedule A (2456)	E,	2 Cn
17.	Assurance of Completion for Off-Site Facilities: (a) Escrow Agreement for Incomplete Off-Site Facilities (2446) with Schedule "A"	E,	2 Cn
18.	Mortgagor's Oath (2478), None in 232	Or,	2 Cn
19.	Mortgagor's Attorney's Opinion	E,	2 Cn
20.	Contractor's Prevailing Wage Certificate (2403-A)	Or,	2 Cn
21.	Chattel Mortgage, or Security Agreement and Financing Statement or Attorney's Opinion that neither are necessary	3 Cn	
22.	Request for Endorsement of Credit Instrument, Certificate of Mortgagor and Mortgagee (2455)	Or,	2 Cn
**23.	Contractor's Certification (2482)	Or,	2 Cn
**24.	Agreement and Certification (3305-A) for 207 or (3306-A) for 220 and 221 (d)(4)	Or,	2 Cn
25.	Sponsor's Certification (3437) for 231-NP and 232-NP	Or,	2 Cn
26.	Guaranty Agreement (3436) for 231-NP and 232-NP if subsidized	E,	2 Cn
27.	For 232 projects: (a) Instrument evidencing acquisition of equipment, if any (e.g. lease, conditional sale contract etc.)	3 Cn	
	(b) Chattel Mortgage on Mortgagor's Interest in equipment	3 Cn	

** To have been filed with Director before start of construction.

PART C. FINAL CLOSING IN CASES OF INSURANCE OF ADVANCES

In these cases, the documents required for initial closing have, of course, been obtained. There will, however, be required these additional documents at final closing:

*** 1.	(a) The Increase Note	3 Cn	
	(b) The Increase Mortgage	3 Cn	
	(c) The Consolidation Agreement or	3 Cn	
	New Note and Mortgage for the total	3 Cn	
*** 2.	Mortgagor's Attorney's Opinion as to Increase	E,	2 Cn
3.	Chattel Mortgage or Security Agreement and Financing Statement or	3 Cn	
	Attorney's Opinion that neither are necessary	Or,	2 Cn
4.	New Title Policy or Original Title Policy brought up to date	E,	2 Cn
5.	Survey showing completed project	3 Cn	
6.	Surveyor's Certificate (2457)	Or,	2 Cn
7.	Escrow Deposit Agreement for incomplete on-site improvements (2456) with Schedule "A"	E,	2 Cn
8.	Assurance of Completion of Off-Site Facilities (a) Escrow Deposit Agreement (2446) with Schedule "A" or	E,	2 Cn
	(b) Off-Site Bond (2479)	E,	2 Cn
9.	Contractor's Prevailing Wage Certificate (2403-A)	Or,	2 E
10.	Request for Final Endorsement of Credit Instrument (2023)	Or,	2 Cn
11.	For 232 projects: (a) Instrument evidencing acquisition of equipment, if any (e.g. lease, conditional sales contract, etc.)	3 Cn	
	(b) Chattel Mortgage on Mortgagor's Interest in equipment	3 Cn	

*** Required only if increase is involved.

50925-P Rev. 4/66   HUD-Wash., D. C

APPENDIX 2

MORTGAGE PAYMENT ESTIMATION CHART

INTEREST RATE (%)	10 YEARS	15 YEARS	20 YEARS	25 YEARS	30 YEARS
5.00	$10.61	$7.91	$6.60	$5.85	$ 5.37
5.25	$10.73	$8.04	$6.74	$5.99	$5.52
5.50	$10.85	$8.17	$6.88	$6.14	$5.68
5.75	$10.98	$8.30	$7.02	$6.29	$5.84
6.00	$11.10	$8.44	$7.16	$6.44	$6.00
6.25	$11.23	$8.57	$7.31	$6.60	$6.16
6.50	$11.35	$8.71	$7.46	$6.75	$6.32
6.75	$11.48	$8.85	$7.60	$6.91	$6.49
7.00	$11.61	$8.99	$7.75	$7.07	$6.65
7.25	$11.74	$9.13	$7.90	$7.23	$6.82
7.50	$11.87	$9.27	$8.06	$7.39	$6.99
7.75	$12.00	$9.41	$8.21	$7.55	$7.16
8.00	$12.13	$9.56	$8.36	$7.72	$7.34
8.25	$12.27	$9.70	$8.52	$7.88	$7.51
8.50	$12.40	$9.85	$8.68	$8.05	$7.69
8.75	$12.53	$9.99	$8.84	$8.22	$7.87
9.00	$12.67	$10.14	$9.00	$8.39	$8.05
9.25	$12.80	$10.29	$9.16	$8.56	$8.23
9.50	$12.94	$10.44	$9.32	$8.74	$8.41
9.75	$13.08	$10.59	$9.49	$8.91	$8.59
10.00	$13.22	$10.75	$9.65	$9.09	$8.78

DIRECTIONS FOR ESTIMATING MONTHLY MORTGAGE PAYMENTS

Select the interest rate and term for the mortgage loan you are considering to ascertain your monthly payment per $1000 of loan principal. For example, if you are considering a mortgage loan in the amount of $50,000 which carries an interest rate of 7.50% for a term of 30 years, multiply the indicated amount of $6.99 by 50 ($50,000/100). Thus, $349.50 is the estimated monthly payment not including taxes, insurance or miscellaneous closing costs.

APPENDIX 3

ADJUSTABLE RATE NOTE

NOTICE TO BORROWER: THIS NOTE CONTAINS A PROVISION ALLOWING FOR CHANGES IN THE INTEREST RATE. INCREASES IN THE INTEREST RATE WILL RESULT IN HIGHER PAYMENTS. DECREASES IN THE INTEREST RATE WILL RESULT IN LOWER PAYMENTS.

HOUSTON HARRIS COUNTY, TEXAS

........................., 19 ....

City   State

....

Property Address   City   State   Zip Code

1. BORROWER'S PROMISE TO PAY

In return for a loan that I have received, I promise to pay U.S. $..................(THIS amount will be called "principal"), plus interest, to order of the Lender. The Lender is

....

....

I understand that the Lender may transfer THIS Note. The Lender or anyone who takes THIS Note by transfer and who is entitled to receive payments under THIS Note will be called the "Note Holder".

2. INTEREST

Interest will be charged on that part of outstanding principal which has not been paid. Interest will be charged beginning on the date I receive principal and continuing until the full amount of principal I receive has been paid.

Beginning on the date of THIS Note, I will pay interest at a yearly rate of ....% (the "Initial Interest Rate"). The interest rate that I will pay will change in accordance with Section 4 of THIS Note until my loan is paid. Interest rate changes may occur on the ...... day of the month beginning on ...., 19............ and on that day of the Month every ....months thereafter. Each date on which the rate of interest may change will be called a "Change Date".

3. PAYMENTS

(A) Time and Place of Payments

I will pay principal and interest by making payments every month. I will make my monthly payments on the ....1st day of each month beginning on

.................................,19......... I will make these payments until I have paid all of the principal and interest and any other charges, described below, that I may owe under THIS Note. I will pay all sums that I owe under THIS Note no later than .... (the "final payment date").

I will make my monthly payments at ....
.... or at a different place if required by the Note Holder. (B) Borrower's Payment Before They Are Due

I have the right to make payments of principal at any time before they are due. A payment of principal only is known as a "prepayment". When I make a prepayment, I will tell the Note Holder in writing that I am doing so. I may make a full prepayment or a partial prepayment without paying any penalty. The Note Holder will use all of my prepayments to reduce the amount of principal that I owe under THIS Note. If I make a partial prepayment, there will be no delays in the due dates of my monthly payments unless the Note Holder agrees in writing to those delays. My partial prepayment will reduce the amount of my monthly payments after the first Change Date following my partial prepayment. However, any reduction due to my partial prepayment may be offset by an interest rate increase.

Amount of Monthly Payments

My initial monthly payments will be in the amount of U.S. $..................... If the interest rate that I pay changes, the amount of my monthly payments will change. Increases in the interest rate will result in higher payments (unless my prepayments since the last Change Date offset the increases in my monthly payments). Decreases in the interest rate will result in lower payments. The amount of my monthly payments will always be sufficient to repay my loan in full in substantially equal payments be the final payment date. In setting the monthly payment amount on each Change Date, the Note Holder will assume that the Note interest rate will no change again prior to the final payment date.

4. INTEREST RATE CHANGES

(A) The Index

Any changes in the interest rate will be based on changes in an interest rate index which will be called the "Index". The Index is the : (Check one box to indicate Index.)

(1) "Contract Interest Rate, Purchase of Previously Occupied Homes, National Average for all Major Types of Lenders "published by the Federal Home Loan Bank Board.

(2)   ....
....

If the Index ceases to be made available by the publisher, or by any successor to the publisher, the Note Holder will set the Note interest rate by using a comparable index.

TEXAS-ADJUSTABLE RATE LOAN NOTE

APPENDIX 4

SAMPLE SPLIT RATE MORTGAGE CLAUSE

FOR VALUE RECEIVED, We, the undersigned, the Promissors and Mortgagors, jointly and severally promise and agree as follows:

To pay to the order of HOME SAVINGS AND LOAN ASSOCIATION, Promisee and Mortgagee, a New York corporation, hereinafter called the "Association," at its offices at New York, New York, or at such other place as may be designated by the holder of the mortgage note, the principal sum of *[Insert Amount]* Dollars ($), and such additional sums as may be subsequently advanced to the Promissors and Mortgagors by the Association, together with interest at the rate of *[Insert Rate]* percent (_ %) per annum until *[Insert Date]* and *[Insert Rate]* percent (%) per annum for the remaining term of the loan, or until the loan shall have been fully paid, subject to the provisions hereinafter set forth.

Such principal and interest shall be due and payable in monthly installments of *[Insert Amount]* Dollars ($) per month, until *[Insert Date]* and *[Insert Amount]* Dollars ($) per month thereafter, subject to the provisions hereinafter set forth. Payments shall be due on the first day of each and every month, commencing *[Insert Date]*.

Notwithstanding any other provisions in this note or the mortgage given as collateral security therefor, the entire sum due hereon, including any additional advances, shall be paid within the time prescribed by law.

APPENDIX 5

TRUTH-IN-LENDING DISCLOSURE STATEMENT

TRUTH-IN-LENDING DISCLOSURE STATEMENT
(THIS IS NEITHER A CONTRACT NOR A COMMITMENT TO LEND)

LENDER OR LENDER'S AGENT: [X] Preliminary [ ] Final

DATE: 08/31/99
LOAN NO.:
Type of Loan: ADJUSTABLE RATE

BORROWERS:

ADDRESS:
CITY/STATE/ZIP:
PROPERTY:

ANNUAL PERCENTAGE RATE The cost of your credit as a yearly rate.	FINANCE CHARGE The dollar amount the credit will cost you.	Amount Financed The amount of credit provided to you or on your behalf.	Total of Payments The amount you will have paid after you have made all payments are scheduled.
e 12.013 %	$ 275,357.44 e	$ 97,413.20 e	$ 372,770.64 e

PAYMENT SCHEDULE:

NUMBER OF PAYMENTS	AMOUNT OF PAYMENTS	PAYMENTS ARE DUE BEGINNING	NUMBER OF PAYMENTS	AMOUNT OF PAYMENTS	PAYMENTS ARE DUE BEGINNING
36	e 896.10	Monthly beginning 11/01/99			
324	e 1,050.96	Monthly beginning 11/01/02			

DEMAND FEATURE: [X] This loan does not have a Demand Feature   [ ] This loan has a Demand Feature

VARIABLE RATE FEATURE:

[X] This loan has a Variable Rate. Variable Rate Disclosures have been provided to you earlier.

SECURITY: You are giving a security interest in the property located at:

ASSUMPTION: Someone buying this property [X] cannot assume the remaining balance due under original mortgage terms
[ ] may assume, subject to lender's conditions, the remaining balance due under original loan terms.

FILING / RECORDING FEES: $ 87.00

PROPERTY INSURANCE: Property hazard insurance in the amount of $ 100,000.00 with a mortgagee clause to the Lender is a required condition of this loan. Borrower may purchase this insurance from any insurance company acceptable to the Lender. Hazard insurance [ ] is [X] is not available through the lender at an estimated cost of for a year term.

LATE CHARGES: If your payment is more than fifteen days late after your due date, you will be charged a late charge of 2.000 % of the overdue payment.

PREPAYMENT: If you pay off your loan early, you
[ ] may [X] will not have to pay a penalty.
[ ] may [X] will not be entitled to a refund of part of the finance charge.

See your contract documents for any additional information regarding non-payment, default, required repayment in full before the scheduled date, and prepayment refunds and penalties.
e means an estimate

I/We hereby acknowledge reading and receiving a complete copy of this disclosure.

_____
BORROWER/DATE

_____
BORROWER/DATE

_____
BORROWER/DATE

_____
BORROWER/DATE

TILI (Rev. 7/98)

APPENDIX 6

NOTICE OF RIGHT TO CANCEL

BORROWER'S NAME	ACCOUNT NUMBER	TYPE OF TRANSACTION

Your Right to Cancel

You are entering into a transaction that will result in a deed of trust or mortgage on your home. You have a legal right under federal law to cancel this transaction, without cost, within three business days from whichever of the following events occurs last:

(1) the date of the transaction which is _____; or

(2) the date you received your Truth in Landing disclosures; or

(3) the date you received this notice of your right to cancel.

If you cancel the transaction, the deed of trust or mortgage is also canceled. Unless modified by court order, within 20 calendar days after we receive your notice, we must take the steps necessary to reflect the fact that the deed of trust or mortgage on your home has been canceled, and we must return to you any money or property you have given to us or to anyone else in connection with this transaction.

Unless modified by court order, you may keep any money we have given you until we have done the things mentioned above, but you must then offer tho return the money. Money must be returned to the address below. If we do not take possession of the money within 20 calendar days of your offer, you must keep it without further obligation.

How to Cancel

If you decide to cancel this transaction, you may do so by notifying us in writing at

_____

_____

(Name & Address of Branch)

You may use any written statement that is signed and dated by you and states your intention to cancel, or you may use this notice by dating and signing below. Keep one copy of this notice because it contains important information about your rights.

If you cancel by mail or telegram, you must send the notice no later than midnight of

_____

(Date)

(Or midnight of the third business day following the latest of the three events listed above). If you send or deliver your written notice to cancel some other way, it must be delivered to the above address no later than that time.

I WISH TO CANCEL

_____   _____

Consumer's Signature   Date

Acknowledgment of Receipt: Each of the undersigned hereby acknowledges receipt of two copies of this "Notice of Right to Cancel."

Date_____

_____   _____

Signature   Signature ORIGINAL

APPENDIX 7

DIRECTORY OF
STATE BANKING AGENCIES

Alabama Superintendent of Banks
Center for Commerce
401 Adams Avenue, Suite #680
Montgomery, AL 36130-1201
Phone: 334-242-3452
Fax: 334-242-3500

Alaska Director of Banking
Department of Commerce
P.O. Box 110807
Juneau, AK 99811-0807
Phone: 907-465-2521
Fax: 907-465- 2549
E-mail: DBSC@COM-
MERCE.STATE.AK.US

Arizona Superintendent of Banks
Arizona State Banking Dept.
2910 North 44th Street, Suite 310
Phoenix, AZ 85018
Phone: 602- 255-4421/1-800-352-8400
Fax: 602-381-1225

Arkansas, Bank Commissioner
Tower Building
323 Center Street, Suite 500
Little Rock, AR 72201-2613
Phone: 501-324-9019
Fax: 501-324-9028

California Department of Financial Institu-
tions
111 Pine Street, Suite 1100
San Francisco, CA 94111-5613
Phone: 415-263-8507/1-800-622-0620
Fax: 415-989- 5310
Website: www.dfi.ca.gov

Colorado, State Bank Commissioner
Division of Banking
1560 Broadway Street, Suite 1175
Denver, CO 80202
Phone: 303-894- 7575
Fax: 303-894-7570
Website: www.dora.state.co.us/banking

Connecticut, Banking Commissioner
Connecticut Department of Banking
260 Constitution Plaza
Hartford, CT 06103
Phone: 860-240- 8100/1-800-831-7225
Fax: 860-240-8178
E-mail: john.burke@po.state.ct.us
Website: www.state.ct.us/dob

Delaware, State Bank Commissioner
555 E. Lockerman Street, Suite 210
Dover, DE 19901
Phone: 302-739-4235
Fax: 302-739-3609

District of Columbia
Superintendent of Banking
and Financial Institutions
717 14th Street, N.W., 11th Floor
Washington, DC 20005
Phone: 202-727-1563
Fax: 202-727-1588
E-mail: jromero@yahoo.com
Website: www.obfi.dcgov.org

Florida, State Comptroller
State Capitol
Tallahassee, FL 32399-0350
Phone: 904-488-0370/1-800-848-3792
Fax: 904-488-9818
E-mail: dbf@mail.dbf.state.fl.us,
Website: www.dbf.state.fl.us/banking.html

Georgia, Commissioner
Banking and Finance
2990 Brandywine Road, Suite 200
Atlanta, GA 30341-5565
Phone: 770-986-1633

Commissioner, Financial Institutions
State of Hawaii
P.O. Box 2054
Honolulu, HI 96805
Phone: 808-586-2820/1-800- 974-4000
Fax: 808-586-2818
E-mail: DFI@LAVA.NET

Idaho, Department of Finance
700 West State Street, 2nd Floor
Boise, ID 83720-0031
Phone: 208-332-8098/1-888-346-3376,
Fax: 208-334-2216
E-mail: GGEE@FIN.STATE.ID.US
Website: www2.state.id.us

Illinois, Commissioner of Banks and Real
Estate
500 E. Monroe Street
Springfield, IL 62701
Phone: 217-782-3000/312-793-3000
Fax: 217-524-5941
E-mail: BANKS@BRE084r1.state.il.us
Website: www.state.il.us/obr

Indiana, Department of Financial
 Institutions
402 W. Washington Street, Room W-066
Indianapolis, IN 46204- 2759
Phone: 317-232-3955/1-800-382-4880
Fax: 317-232-7655
E-mail: cphillips@dfi.state.in.us

Iowa, Superintendent of Banking
200 East Grand, Suite 300
Des Moines, IA 50309
Phone: 515-281-4014/1-800-972-2018
Fax: 515- 281-4862
Website: www.idob.state.ia.us

Kansas, State Bank Commissioner
700 Jackson Street, Suite 300
Topeka, KS 66603-3714
Phone: 785-296-2266
Fax: 785-296-0168

Kentucky, Department of Financial Institu-
tions
77 Versailles Road
Frankfort, KY 40601
Phone: 502-573-3390/1- 800-223-2579
Fax: 502-573-8787
Website: www.dfi.state.ky.us

Louisiana, Commissioner, Financial Institu-
tions
P.O. Box 94095
Baton Rouge, LA 70804-9095
Phone: 504-925-4660
Fax: 504- 925-4524

Maine, Superintendent of Banking
36 State House Station
Augusta, ME 04333-0036
Phone: 207-624-8570
Fax: 207-624-8590
Website: www.state.me.us

Maryland, Commissioner of Financial
Regulation
500 North Calvert Street
Baltimore, MD 21202
Phone: 410-333-6812/1-888- 784-0136
Fax: 410-333-0475
E-mail: fin-reg@dllr.state.md.us
Website: www.dllr.state.md.us/finance

Massachusetts, Commissioner of Banks
100 Cambridge Street
Boston, MA 02202
Phone: 617-727-3145/1-800-495-2265
Fax: 617-727- 7631

Michigan, Commissioner, Financial
Institutions Bureau
P.O. Box 30224
Lansing, MI 48909
Phone: 517-373-3460, 515-335-1109

Fax: 517-335-0908
Website: www.cis.state.mi.us

Minnesota, Deputy Commissioner
Enforcement and Licensing Division
133 East 7th Street
St. Paul, MN 55101
Phone: 612-296- 2135/1-800-657-3602
Fax: 612-296-8591

Mississippi, Commissioner, Department of
Banking
and Consumer Finance
P.O. Box 23729
Jackson, MS 39225-3729
Phone: 601-359-1031/1-800-844-2499
Fax: 601-359-3557

Missouri, Commissioner of Finance
P.O. Box 716
Jefferson City, MO 65102
Phone: 573-751-3242
Fax: 573-751-9192
E-mail: finance@mail.state.mo.us

Montana, Commissioner, Financial Institu-
tions
846 Front Street
P.O. Box 200546
Helena, MT 59620-0546
Phone: 406-444- 2091
Fax: 406-444-4186

Nebraska, Director of Banking and Finance
1200 N Street, Suite 311
Lincoln, NE 68508
Phone: 402-471-2171
Fax: 402-471-3062
Website: www.ndbf.org

Nevada, Commissioner, Financial Institu-
tions
406 East Second Street, Suite 3
Carson City, NV 89701-4758
Phone: 702-687-4259
Fax: 702-687-6909

New Hampshire
Bank Commissioner
169 Manchester Street
Concord, NH 03301
Phone: 603-271-3561
Fax: 603-271-1090

New Jersey, Commissioner
Department of Banking and Insurance
20 West State Street
P.O. Box 040
Trenton, NJ 08625
Phone: 609-292-3420

New Mexico
Financial Institutions Division
P.O. Box 25101

Santa Fe, NM 87504
Phone: 505-827-7100
Fax: 505-827-7107

New York, Superintendent of Banking
New York State Banking Department
Two Rector Street, New York, NY
10006-1894
 Phone: 212-618-6553/1-800-522-3330

North Carolina, Commissioner of Banks
P.O. Box 10709
Raleigh, NC 27605
Phone: 919-733-3016
Fax: 919-733-6918
Website: www.banking.state.nc.us

North Dakota, Commissioner of
Banking and Financial Institutions
2000 Schafer Street
Bismarck, ND 58501-1204
Phone: 701-328-9933
Fax: 701-328-9955
E-mail: banking@BTIGATE.com
Website: www.state.nd.us/bank

Ohio, Superintendent, Division of
Financial Institutions
77 South High Street, 21st Floor
Columbus, OH 43266-0121
Phone: 614- 644-1631

Oklahoma, Bank Commissioner
4545 North Lincoln Blvd., Suite 164
Oklahoma City, OK 73105
Phone: 405-521-2782
Fax: 405-525-9701
Website: www.state.ok.us

Oregon, Division of
Finance and Corporate Securities
350 Winter Street, NE, Room 21
Salem, OR 97310
Phone: 503-378-4140
Fax: 503-947-7862
Website: www.cbs.state.or.us/external/dfcs

Pennsylvania, Secretary of Banking
333 Market Street, 16th Floor
Harrisburg, PA 17101-2290
Phone: 717-787-6991/1-800-PA- BANKS
Fax: 717-787-8773

Puerto Rico, Commissioner of
Financial Institutions
1492 Ponce de Leon Avenue, Suite 600
San Juan, PR 00907-4127
Phone: 787- 723-3131
Fax: 787-723-4042

Rhode Island, Superintendent of Banking
233 Richmond Street, Suite 231
Providence, RI 02903-4231

Phone: 401-277-2405
Fax: 401-331-9123

South Carolina, Commissioner of Banking
1015 Sumter Street, Room 309
Columbia, SC 29201
Phone: 803-734-2001
Fax: 803-734- 2013

South Dakota, Director of Banking
State Capitol Building
500 East Capitol Avenue
Pierre, SD 57501-5070
Phone: 605-773-3421
Fax: 605-773-5367

Tennessee, Commissioner
Financial Institutions
John Sevier Building
500 Charlotte Avenue, 4th Floor
Nashville, TN 37243-0705
Phone: 615-741-2236
Fax: 615-741-2883
E-mail: tsmith@mail.state.tn.us

Texas, Banking Commissioner
2601 North Lamar
Austin, TX 78705
Phone: 512-475-1300
Fax: 512-475-3300,
Website: www.banking.state.tx.us

Utah, Commissioner, Financial Institutions
P.O. Box 89
Salt Lake City, UT 84110-0089
Phone: 801-538-8854
Fax: 801-538-8894

Vermont, Commissioner
Banking, Insurance, Securities
and Health Care Administration
89 Main Street Drawer 20
Montpelier, VT 05620-3101
Phone: 802-828-3301
Fax: 802-828- 3306
Website: www.state.vt.us/bis

Virgin Islands
Commissioner of Insurance
Chairman of Banking Board
Kongen's Garden #18
Charlotte Amalie, St. Thomas, VI 00802
Phone: 340-774-2991
Fax: 340-774-6953

Virginia, Commissioner, Financial Institu-
tions
1300 E. Main Street, Suite 800
P.O. Box 640
Richmond, VA 23218-0640
Phone: 804-371-9657/1-800-552-7945
Fax: 804-371-9416

Washington, Department of Financial
Institutions
P.O. Box 41200
Olympia, WA 98504-1200
Phone: 360-902-8707
Fax: 360-586- 5068

West Virginia, Commissioner of Banking
State Capitol Complex, Building 3, Room
311
1900 Kanawha Blvd. East
Charleston, WV 25305-0240
Phone: 304-558-2294, 1-800-642-9056

Wisconsin, Department of Financial Institu-
tions
345 W. Washington Ave, 5th Floor
P.O. Box 7876
Madison, WI 53707-7876
Phone: 608-261-9555/1-800-452-3328
Fax: 608-264-7968
E-mail: badger.state.wi.us/agencies/dfi

Wyoming, Division of Banking
Herschler Building, 3rd Floor East
Cheyenne, WY 82002
Phone: 307-777-7797
Fax: 307-777- 3555

APPENDIX 8

SAMPLE GOOD FAITH ESTIMATE

GOOD FAITH ESTIMATE

Loan Number:
Lender:

Address:

Applicant(s):

Property Address:

Sales Price:
Base Loan Amount: 100,000.00
Total Loan Amount: 100,000.00
Type of Loan: ADJUSTABLE RATE
Date Prepared: 08/31/99
Rate: 10.250 %   Term: 360 MONTHS

The information provided below reflects estimates of the charges which you are likely to incur at the settlement of your loan. The fees listed are estimates - the actual charges may be more or less. Your transaction may not involve a fee for every item listed. The numbers listed beside the estimates generally correspond to the numbered lines contained in the HUD-1 or HUD-1A Settlement Statement that you will be receiving at settlement. The HUD-1 or HUD-1A Settlement Statement will show you the actual cost for items paid at settlement. The loan terms and fees may change based on the information gathered during the underwriting and loan approval process or as a result of negotiations between you and the Lender.

" L" designates those costs to be paid outside of closing by Lender.   "S" designates those costs to be paid by Seller.

800 ITEMS PAYABLE IN CONNECTION WITH LOAN:	
801 Loan Origination Fee (%)	$ 0.00
802 Loan Discount Fee (1.500 %)	$ 1,500.00
803 Appraisal Fee $ 245.00 TO $ 360.00	$ 275.00
804 Credit Report $ TO $	$
805 Lender's Inspection Fee	$
806 Mortgage Insurance Application Fee	$
807 Assumption Fee	$
808 Mortgage Broker Fee (TOTAL)	$
809 CLO Access Fee	$
810 Tax Related Service Fee	$ 76.00
811 Flood Search Fee	$ 30.00
812 Lender's Proc Fee	$ 425.00
NY Recording Fee-Lender Portion	$ 250.00
*(Fee not included in funds due from borrower.)	$

900 ITEMS REQUIRED BY LENDER TO BE PAID IN ADVANCE:	
901 Interest for 10 day @ $ 28.08 per day	$ 280.80
902 Mortgage Insurance Premium	$
903 Hazard Insurance Premium	$
	$
	$

1000 RESERVES DEPOSITED WITH LENDER:	
1001 Haz Ins Prem 0 @ $ 50.00	$
Tax & Assmt Res 0 @ $ 333.33	$
	$
	$
	$

TOTAL ESTIMATED FUNDS NEEDED TO CLOSE:	
Downpayment	$
Est. Closing Costs	$ 4,272.00
Est. Prepaid Items/Reserves	$ 280.80
OTHER	$
TOTAL EST. FUNDS NEEDED TO CLOSE	$ 4,552.80
TOTAL FEES PAID BY LENDER	$

1100 TITLE CHARGES:	
1101 Closing or Escrow Fee $ 0.00 TO $ 330.00	$
1102 Abstract or Title Search 110.00 TO 200.00	$ 125.00
1103 Title Examination	$
1104 Title Insurance Binder	$
1105 Document Preparation Fee	$
1106 Notary Fee	$
1107 Attorney Fees $ TO $	$
1108 Title Insurance 715.00 TO 905.00	$ 754.00
	$
	$
	$
	$
	$

1200 GOVERNMENT RECORDING AND TRANSFER CHARGES:	
1201 Recording Fees:	$ 87.00
1202 City/County Tax/Stamps:	$
1203	$
1204 NY Recording Fee	$ 725.00
1205	$
	$

1300 ADDITIONAL SETTLEMENT CHARGES:	
1301 Survey	$
1302 Pest Inspection	$
	$
	$
	$
1306	$
1307 APPLICATION FEE	$ 275.00
TOTAL ESTIMATED SETTLEMENT CHARGES	$ 4,552.80
TOTAL SETTLEMENT CHARGES PAID BY LENDER	$

TOTAL ESTIMATED MONTHLY PAYMENT	
Principal & Interest	$ 896.10
Real Estate Taxes	$
Flood & Hazard Insurance	$
Mortgage Insurance	$
TOTAL MONTHLY PAYMENT	$ 896.10

THIS SECTION TO BE COMPLETED BY LENDER ONLY IF A PARTICULAR PROVIDER OF SERVICE IS REQUIRED. Use of the particular provider is required and the estimate is based on charges of the provider. If a particular provider is not mentioned, a provider will be required from a lender approved list.

ITEM NO.	NAME & ADDRESS OF PROVIDER	TELEPHONE NO.	NATURE OF RELATIONSHIP
803	Appraisal Repeated Use		Unaffiliated/Repeated Use
804	Credit Repeated Use		Unaffiliated/Repeated Use
1108	Title Company Repeated Use		Unaffiliated/Repeated Use
1101	Closing Agent Repeated Use		Unaffiliated/Repeated Use
811	PINNACLE DATA CORP		Unaffiliated/Used 100%/Flood
810	FIDELITY NATIONAL TAX SERVICE		Unaffiliated/Used 100%/Tax

These estimates are provided pursuant to the Real Estate Settlement Procedures Act of 1974, as amended (RESPA). Additional information can be found in the HUD Special Information Booklet, which is to be provided to you by your mortgage broker or lender, if your application is to purchase residential real property and the Lender will take a first lien on the property. The undersigned acknowledges receipt of the booklet "Settlement Costs," and the Consumer Handbook on ARM Mortgages, if applicable.

Applicant	Date	Applicant	Date

Applicant	Date	Applicant	Date

☐   This Good Faith Estimate is being provided by _____ , a mortgage broker, and no lender has yet been obtained.

OFFICER B (1/99)

APPENDIX 9

SAMPLE RESPA SERVICING DISCLOSURE FORM

08/31/99 —————— RESPA SERVICING DISCLOSURE —— LOAN NO. ——— ——

Lender:

NOTICE TO FIRST LIEN MORTGAGE LOAN APPLICANTS: THE RIGHT TO COLLECT YOUR MORTGAGE LOAN PAYMENTS MAY BE TRANSFERRED. FEDERAL LAW GIVES YOU CERTAIN RELATED RIGHTS. IF YOUR LOAN IS MADE, SAVE THIS STATEMENT WITH YOUR LOAN DOCUMENTS. SIGN THE ACKNOWLEDGMENT AT THE END OF THIS STATEMENT ONLY IF YOU UNDERSTAND ITS CONTENTS.

Because you are applying for a mortgage loan covered by the Real Estate Settlement Procedures Act (RESPA) (12 U.S.C. Section 2601 et seq.) you have certain rights under that Federal law.

This Statement tells you about all those rights. It also tells you what the chances are that the servicing for this loan may be transferred to a different loan servicer. "Servicing" refers to collecting your principal, interest and escrow account payments, if any. If your loan servicer changes, there are certain procedures that must be followed. This statement generally explains those procedures.

Transfer Practices and Requirements

If the servicing of your loan is assigned, sold, or transferred to a new servicer, you must be given written notice of that transfer. The present loan servicer must send you notice in writing of the assignment, sale or transfer of the servicing not less than 15 days before the effective date of the transfer. The new loan servicer must also send you notice within 15 days after the effective date of the transfer. The present servicer and the new servicer may combine this information in one notice, so long as the notice is sent to you 15 days before the effective date of transfer. The 15 day period is not applicable if a notice of prospective transfer is provided to you at settlement. The law allows a delay in the time (not more than 30 days after the transfer) for servicers to notify you, upon the occurrence of certain business emergencies.

Notices must contain certain information. They must contain the effective date of the transfer of the servicing of your loan to the new servicer, and the name, address, and toll-free or collect call telephone number of the new servicer, and toll-free or collect call telephone numbers of a person or department for both your present servicer and your new servicer to answer your questions. During the 60-day period following the effective date of the transfer of the loan servicing, a loan payment received by your old servicer before its due date may not be treated by the new loan servicer as late, and a late fee may not be imposed on you.

Complaint Resolution

Section 6 of RESPA (12 U.S.C. Section 2605) gives you certain consumer rights, *whether or not your loan servicing is transferred.* If you send a "qualified written request" to your servicer, your servicer must provide you with a written acknowledgment within 20 Business Days of receipt of your request. A "qualified written request" is a written correspondence, other than notice on a payment coupon or other payment medium supplied by the servicer, which includes your name and account number, and the information regarding your request. Not later than 60 Business Days after receiving your request, your servicer must make any appropriate corrections to your account, or must provide you with a written clarification regarding any dispute. During this 60-Business Day period, your servicer may not provide information to a consumer reporting agency concerning any overdue payment related to such period or qualified written request.

A Business Day is any day in which the offices of the business entity are open to the public for carrying on substantially all of its business functions.

Damages and Costs

Section 6 of RESPA also provides for damages and costs for individuals or classes of individuals in circumstances where servicers are shown to have violated the requirements of that Section.

Servicing Transfer Estimates

1. The following is the best estimate of what will happen to the servicing of your mortgage loan:

☐ We may assign, sell or transfer the servicing of your loan while the loan is outstanding. ☒ We are able to service your loan and we ☐ will ☐ will not ☒ haven't decided whether to service your loan.
OR

☐ We do not service mortgage loans, ☐ and we have not serviced mortgage loans in the past three years. ☐ We presently intend to assign, sell or transfer the servicing of your mortgage loan. You will be informed about your servicer.

☐ We assign, sell or transfer the servicing of some of our loans while the loan is outstanding depending on the type of loan or other factors. For the program you have applied for, we expect to:
☐ sell all of the mortgage servicing ☐ retain all of the mortgage servicing
☐ assign, sell or transfer _____ % of the mortgage servicing

2. For all the first lien mortgage loans that we make in the 12-month period after your mortgage loan is funded, we estimate that the percentage of mortgage loans for which we will transfer servicing is between:
_X_ [0 to 25%] or [NONE] _____ 26 to 50% _____ 51 to 75% _____ [76 to 100%] or [ALL]
This estimate ☒ does ☐ does not include assignments, sales or transfers to affiliates or subsidiaries. This is only our best estimate and it is not binding. Business conditions or other circumstances may affect our future transferring decisions.

3. ☒ We have previously assigned, sold or transferred the servicing of first lien mortgage loans

This information ☒ does ☐ does not include assignments, sales or transfers to affiliates or subsidiaries.

_____   _____ —— —— —— — —— ——
Date   Present Servicer or Lender

ACKNOWLEDGMENT OF MORTGAGE LOAN APPLICANT
I/We have read this disclosure form and understand its contents, as evidenced by my/our signature(s) below. I/We understand that this acknowledgment is a required part of the mortgage loan application.

_____ _____   _____ _____
Applicant   Date   Applicant   Date

_____ _____   _____ _____
Applicant   Date   Applicant   Date

SERVICING1 (REV 6/99)

APPENDIX 10

HUD-1 SETTLEMENT STATEMENT

A. **Settlement Statement**

U.S. Department of Housing and Urban Development

OMB Approval No. 2502-0265

B. Type of Loan

	6. File Number:	7. Loan Number:	8. Mortgage Insurance Case Number:
1. ☐ FHA 2. ☐ FmHA -3. ☐ Conv. Unins.			
4. ☐ VA 5. ☐ Conv. Ins.			

C. Note: This form is furnished to give you a statement of actual settlement costs. Amounts paid to and by the settlement agent are shown. Items marked "(p.o.c.)" were paid outside the closing; they are shown here for informational purposes and are not included in the totals.

D. Name & Address of Borrower:	E. Name & Address of Seller:	F. Name & Address of Lender:

G. Property Location:	H. Settlement Agent:	
	Place of Settlement:	I. Settlement Date:

J. Summary of Borrower's Transaction		K. Summary of Seller's Transaction	
100. Gross Amount Due From Borrower		**400. Gross Amount Due To Seller**	
101. Contract sales price		401. Contract sales price	
102. Personal property		402. Personal property	
103. Settlement charges to borrower (line 1400)		403.	
104.		404.	
105.		405.	
Adjustments for items paid by seller in advance		**Adjustments for items paid by seller in advance**	
106. City/town taxes to		406. City/town taxes to	
107. County taxes to		407. County taxes to	
108. Assessments to		408. Assessments to	
109.		409.	
110.		410.	
111.		411.	
112.		412.	
120. Gross Amount Due From Borrower		**420. Gross Amount Due To Seller**	
200. Amounts Paid By Or In Behalf Of Borrower		**500. Reductions In Amount Due To Seller**	
201. Deposit or earnest money		501. Excess deposit (see instructions)	
202. Principal amount of new loan(s)		502. Settlement charges to seller (line 1400)	
203. Existing loan(s) taken subject to		503. Existing loan(s) taken subject to	
204.		504. Payoff of first mortgage loan	
205.		505. Payoff of second mortgage loan	
206.		506.	
207.		507.	
208.		508.	
209.		509.	
Adjustments for items unpaid by seller		**Adjustments for items unpaid by seller**	
210. City/town taxes to		510. City/town taxes to	
211. County taxes to		511. County taxes to	
212. Assessments to		512. Assessments to	
213.		513.	
214.		514.	
215.		515.	
216.		516.	
217.		517.	
218.		518.	
219.		519.	
220. Total Paid By/For Borrower		**520. Total Reduction Amount Due Seller**	
300. Cash At Settlement From/To Borrower		**600. Cash At Settlement To/From Seller**	
301. Gross Amount due from borrower (line 120)		601. Gross amount due to seller (line 420)	
302. Less amounts paid by/for borrower (line 220)	( )	602. Less reductions in amt. due seller (line 520)	( )
303. Cash ☐ From ☐ To Borrower		**603. Cash** ☐ To ☐ From Seller	

Section 5 of the Real Estate Settlement Procedures Act (RESPA) requires the following: • HUD must develop a Special Information Booklet to help persons borrowing money to finance the purchase of residential real estate to better understand the nature and costs of real estate settlement services; • Each lender must provide the booklet to all applicants from whom it receives or for whom it prepares a written application to borrow money to finance the purchase of residential real estate; • Lenders must prepare and distribute with the Booklet a Good Faith Estimate of the settlement costs that the borrower is likely to incur in connection with the settlement. These disclosures are mandatory.

Section 4(a) of RESPA mandates that HUD develop and prescribe this standard form to be used at the time of loan settlement to provide full disclosure of all charges imposed upon the borrower and seller. These are third party disclosures that are designed to provide the borrower with pertinent information during the settlement process in order to be a better shopper.

The Public Reporting Burden for this collection of information is estimated to average one hour per response, including the time for reviewing instructions, searching existing data sources, gathering and maintaining the data needed, and completing and reviewing the collection of information.

This agency may not collect this information, and you are not required to complete this form, unless it displays a currently valid OMB control number.

The information requested does not lend itself to confidentiality.

L. Settlement Charges

		Paid From Borrowers Funds at Settlement	Paid From Seller's Funds at Settlement
700. Total Sales/Broker's Commission based on price $ @ % =			
Division of Commission (line 700) as follows:			
701. $ to			
702. $ to			
703. Commission paid at Settlement			
704.			
800. Items Payable In Connection With Loan			
801. Loan Origination Fee %			
802. Loan Discount %			
803. Appraisal Fee to			
804. Credit Report to			
805. Lender's Inspection Fee			
806. Mortgage Insurance Application Fee to			
807. Assumption Fee			
808.			
809.			
810.			
811.			
900. Items Required By Lender To Be Paid In Advance			
901. Interest from to @ $ /day			
902. Mortgage Insurance Premium for months to			
903. Hazard Insurance Premium for years to			
904. years to			
905.			
1000. Reserves Deposited With Lender			
1001. Hazard insurance months @ $ per month			
1002. Mortgage insurance months @ $ per month			
1003. City property taxes months @ $ per month			
1004. County property taxes months @ $ per month			
1005. Annual assessments months @ $ per month			
1006. months @ $ per month			
1007. months @ $ per month			
1008. months @ $ per month			
1100. Title Charges			
1101. Settlement or closing fee to			
1102. Abstract or title search to			
1103. Title examination to			
1104. Title insurance binder to			
1105. Document preparation to			
1106. Notary fees to			
1107. Attorney's fees to			
(includes above items numbers:)			
1108. Title insurance to			
(includes above items numbers:)			
1109. Lender's coverage $			
1110. Owner's coverage $			
1111.			
1112.			
1113.			
1200. Government Recording and Transfer Charges			
1201. Recording fees: Deed $; Mortgage $; Releases $			
1202. City/county tax/stamps: Deed $; Mortgage $			
1203. State tax/stamps: Deed $; Mortgage $			
1204.			
1205.			
1300. Additional Settlement Charges			
1301. Survey to			
1302. Pest inspection to			
1303.			
1304.			
1305.			
1400. Total Settlement Charges (enter on lines 103, Section J and 502, Section K)			

APPENDIX 11

CLOSING COST ESTIMATOR
BUYERS ESTIMATED
CLOSING COSTS

Item	Estimated Amount	Actual Amount
(1) - Application Fee	Charged by Lender, May range from $100 - $300	$_____
(2) - Appraisal Fee	Approximately $250	$_____
(3) - Credit Report	Approximately $50	$_____
(4) - Escrow Fees (Insurance)	Amounts paid to lender for insurance Generally includes advance payments of homeowner's insurance (2 months); and flood and PMI insurance, when required (2 months)	$_____
(5) - Escrow Fees (Taxes)	Amounts paid to lender for property and school taxes, Generally includes advance (3 months)	$_____
(6) - Flood Certification Fee	Required by lender to verify flood zone status of property, Approximately $15.	$_____
(7) - Flood Insurance	Varies depending on flood zone, generally $500 - $1000 per year	$_____
(8) - Funding Fee	A percentage of the loan amount charged on VA loans instead of PMI	$_____
(9) - Home Inspection	Approximately $300 - $500	$_____
(10) - Homeowner's Insurance	Varies, generally .0025 of purchase price per year	$_____
(11) - Buyer's Legal Fees	Legal fees vary depending on attorney and location, but generally range from $750 - $1,000	$_____

Item	Estimated Amount	Actual Amount
(12) - Lender's Legal Fee	For review of documents, Ranges from $150 - $250, where applicable	$_____
(13) - Mortgage Tax	Generally 0.75% of mortgage amount, where applicable	$_____
(14) - Points	Amount paid to lender to "buydown" interest rate on mortgage, usually ranges from 0 to 3 points	$_____
(15) - Prepaid Interest	Interest on mortgage payable to lender from date of closing to end of 1st month	$_____
(16) - Private Mortgage Insurance	PMI is required if mortgage is more than 80% of purchase price, Generally .004 of - mortgage amount	$_____
(17) - Recording Fees	Approximately $50 - $75	$_____
(18) - Survey	Depends on size of property, but ranges from $350 - $500	$_____
(19) - Title Insurance	Approximately $500 per $100,000 of coverage	$_____
(20) - Title Search	Approximately $150 - $200	$_____
Estimated Total Closing Costs:		$_____

APPENDIX 12

UNIFORM RESIDENTIAL LOAN APPLICATION

Uniform Residential Loan Application

This application is designed to be completed by the applicant(s) with the lender's assistance. Applicants should complete this form as "Borrower" or "Co-Borrower", as applicable. Co-Borrower information must also be provided (and the appropriate box checked) when ☐ the income or assets of a person other than the "Borrower" (including the Borrower's spouse) will be used as a basis for loan qualification or ☐ the income or assets of the Borrower's spouse will not be used as a basis for loan qualification, but his or her liabilities must be considered because the Borrower resides in a community property state, the security property is located in a community property state, or the Borrower is relying on other property located in a community property state as a basis for repayment of the loan.

I. TYPE OF MORTGAGE AND TERMS OF LOAN

Mortgage Applied for:	☐ VA ☐ FHA	☐ Conventional ☐ FmHA	☐ Other:	Agency Case Number	Lender Case No.
Amount $	Interest Rate %	No. of Months	Amortization Type:	☐ Fixed Rate ☐ GPM	☐ Other (explain): ☐ ARM (type):

II. PROPERTY INFORMATION AND PURPOSE OF LOAN

Subject Property Address (street, city, state, & ZIP)	No. of Units

Legal Description of Subject Property (attach description if necessary)	Year Built

Purpose of Loan	☐ Purchase ☐ Refinance	☐ Construction ☐ Construction-Permanent	☐ Other (explain):	Property will be: ☐ Primary Residence ☐ Secondary Residence ☐ Investment

Complete this line if construction or construction-permanent loan.

Year Lot Acquired	Original Cost $	Amount Existing Liens $	(a) Present Value of Lot $	(b) Cost of Improvements $	Total (a + b) $

Complete this line if this is a refinance loan.

Year Acquired	Original Cost $	Amount Existing Liens $	Purpose of Refinance	Describe Improvements ☐ made ☐ to be made Cost: $

Title will be held in what Name(s)	Manner in which Title will be held	Estate will be held in: ☐ Fee Simple ☐ Leasehold (show expiration date)

Source of Down Payment, Settlement Charges and/or Subordinate Financing (explain)

III. BORROWER INFORMATION

	Borrower	Co-Borrower
Name	Borrower's Name (include Jr. or Sr. if applicable)	Co-Borrower's Name (include Jr. or Sr. if applicable)

Social Security Number	Home Phone (incl. area code)	Age	Yrs. School	Social Security Number	Home Phone (incl. area code)	Age	Yrs. School

☐ Married ☐ Separated ☐ Unmarried (include single, divorced, widowed)	Dependents (not listed by Co-Borrower) no. ages	☐ Married ☐ Separated ☐ Unmarried (include single, divorced, widowed)	Dependents (not listed by Borrower) no. ages
Present Address (street, city, state, ZIP) ☐ Own ☐ Rent ___ No. Yrs.		Present Address (street, city, state, ZIP) ☐ Own ☐ Rent ___ No. Yrs.	

If residing at present address for less than two years, complete the following:

Former Address (street, city, state, ZIP) ☐ Own ☐ Rent ___ No. Yrs.	Former Address (street, city, state, ZIP) ☐ Own ☐ Rent ___ No. Yrs.
Former Address (street, city, state, ZIP) ☐ Own ☐ Rent ___ No. Yrs.	Former Address (street, city, state, ZIP) ☐ Own ☐ Rent ___ No. Yrs.

IV. EMPLOYMENT INFORMATION

	Borrower	Co-Borrower
Name & Address of Employer	☐ Self Employed	Yrs. on this job	Name & Address of Employer	☐ Self Employed	Yrs. on this job

Name & Address of Employer	☐ Self Employed	Yrs. on this job / Yrs. employed in this line of work/profession	Name & Address of Employer	☐ Self Employed	Yrs. on this job / Yrs. employed in this line of work/profession
Position/Title/Type of Business		Business Phone (incl. area code)	Position/Title/Type of Business		Business Phone (incl. area code)

If employed in current position for less than two years or if currently employed in more than one position, complete the following:

Name & Address of Employer	☐ Self Employed	Dates (from - to)	Name & Address of Employer	☐ Self Employed	Dates (from - to)
		Monthly Income $			Monthly Income $
Position/Title/Type of Business		Business Phone (incl. area code)	Position/Title/Type of Business		Business Phone (incl. area code)
Name & Address of Employer	☐ Self Employed	Dates (from - to)	Name & Address of Employer	☐ Self Employed	Dates (from - to)
		Monthly Income $			Monthly Income $
Position/Title/Type of Business		Business Phone (incl. area code)	Position/Title/Type of Business		Business Phone (incl. area code)

V. MONTHLY INCOME AND COMBINED HOUSING EXPENSE INFORMATION

Gross Monthly Income	Borrower	Co-Borrower	Total	Combined Monthly Housing Expense	Present	Proposed
Base Empl. Income *	$	$	$	Rent	$	
Overtime				First Mortgage (P&I)		$
Bonuses				Other Financing (P&I)		
Commissions				Hazard Insurance		
Dividends/Interest				Real Estate Taxes		
Net Rental Income				Mortgage Insurance		
Other (before completing, see the notice in "describe other income," below)				Homeowner Assn. Dues		
				Other:		
Total	$	$	$	Total	$	$

* Self Employed Borrower(s) may be required to provide additional documentation such as tax returns and financial statements.

Describe Other Income *Notice:* Alimony, child support, or separate maintenance income need not be revealed if the Borrower (B) or Co-Borrower (C) does not choose to have it considered for repaying this loan.

B/C		Monthly Amount
		$

VI. ASSETS AND LIABILITIES

This Statement and any applicable supporting schedules may be completed jointly by both married and unmarried Co-Borrowers if their assets and liabilities are sufficiently joined so that the Statement can be meaningfully and fairly presented on a combined basis; otherwise separate Statements and Schedules are required. If the Co-Borrower section was completed about a spouse, this Statement and supporting schedules must be completed about that spouse also.

Completed ☐ Jointly ☐ Not Jointly

ASSETS Description	Cash or Market Value	Liabilities and Pledged Assets. List the creditor's name, address and account number for all outstanding debts, including automobile loans, revolving charge accounts, real estate loans, alimony, child support, stock pledges, etc. Use continuation sheet, if necessary. Indicate by (*) those liabilities which will be satisfied upon sale of real estate owned or upon refinancing of the subject property.		
Cash deposit toward purchase held by:	$	LIABILITIES	Monthly Payt. & Mos. Left to Pay	Unpaid Balance
List checking and savings accounts below		Name and address of Company	$ Payt./Mos.	$
Name and address of Bank, S&L, or Credit Union				
		Acct. no.		
		Name and address of Company	$ Payt./Mos.	$
Acct. no.	$			
Name and address of Bank, S&L, or Credit Union				
		Acct. no.		
		Name and address of Company	$ Payt./Mos.	$
Acct. no.	$			
Name and address of Bank, S&L, or Credit Union				
		Acct. no.		
		Name and address of Company	$ Payt./Mos.	$
Acct. no.	$			
Name and address of Bank, S&L, or Credit Union				
		Acct. no.		
		Name and address of Company	$ Payt./Mos.	$
Acct. no.	$			
Stocks & Bonds (Company name/number & description)	$			
		Acct. no.		
		Name and address of Company	$ Payt./Mos.	$
Life insurance net cash value	$			
Face amount: $				
Subtotal Liquid Assets	$			
Real estate owned (enter market value from schedule of real estate owned)	$	Acct. no.		
Vested interest in retirement fund	$	Name and address of Company	$ Payt./Mos.	$
Net worth of business(es) owned (attach financial statement)	$			
Automobiles owned (make and year)	$			
		Acct. no.		
		Alimony/Child Support/Separate Maintenance Payments Owed to:	$	
Other Assets (itemize)	$	Job Related Expense (child care, union dues, etc.)	$	
		Total Monthly Payments	$	
Total Assets a.	$		$	Total Liabilities b. $

VI. ASSETS AND LIABILITIES (cont.)

Schedule of Real Estate Owned (If additional properties are owned, use continuation sheet.)

Property Address (enter S if sold, PS if pending sale or R if rental being held for income)	Type of Property	Present Market Value	Amount of Mortgages & Liens	Gross Rental Income	Mortgage Payments	Insurance, Maintenance, Taxes & Misc.	Net Rental Income
		$	$	$	$	$	$
Totals		$	$	$	$	$	$

List any additional names under which credit has previously been received and indicate appropriate creditor name(s) and account number(s):

Alternate Name	Creditor Name	Account Number

VII. DETAILS OF TRANSACTION | ## VIII. DECLARATIONS

VII. DETAILS OF TRANSACTION		VIII. DECLARATIONS	Borrower		Co-Borrower	
		If you answer "yes" to any questions a through i, please use continuation sheet for explanation.	Yes	No	Yes	No
a. Purchase price	$	a. Are there any outstanding judgments against you?	☐	☐	☐	☐
b. Alterations, improvements, repairs		b. Have you been declared bankrupt within the past 7 years?	☐	☐	☐	☐
c. Land (if acquired separately)		c. Have you had property foreclosed upon or given title or deed in lieu thereof in the last 7 years?	☐	☐	☐	☐
d. Refinance (incl. debts to be paid off)						
e. Estimated prepaid items		d. Are you a party to a lawsuit?	☐	☐	☐	☐
f. Estimated closing costs		e. Have you directly or indirectly been obligated on any loan which resulted in foreclosure, transfer of title in lieu of foreclosure, or judgment? (This would include such loans as home mortgage loans, SBA loans, home improvement loans, educational loans, manufactured (mobile) home loans, any mortgage, financial obligation, bond, or loan guarantee. If "Yes," provide details, including date, name and address of Lender, FHA or VA case number, if any, and reasons for the action.)	☐	☐	☐	☐
g. PMI, MIP, Funding Fee						
h. Discount (if Borrower will pay)						
i. Total costs (add items a through h)						
j. Subordinate financing		f. Are you presently delinquent or in default on any Federal debt or any other loan, mortgage, financial obligation, bond, or loan guarantee? If "Yes," give details as described in the preceding question.	☐	☐	☐	☐
k. Borrower's closing costs paid by Seller						
l. Other Credits (explain)		g. Are you obligated to pay alimony, child support, or separate maintenance?	☐	☐	☐	☐
		h. Is any part of the down payment borrowed?	☐	☐	☐	☐
		i. Are you a co-maker or endorser on a note?	☐	☐	☐	☐
		j. Are you a U.S. citizen?	☐	☐	☐	☐
m. Loan amount (exclude PMI, MIP, Funding Fee financed)		k. Are you a permanent resident alien?	☐	☐	☐	☐
		l. Do you intend to occupy the property as your primary residence?	☐	☐	☐	☐
n. PMI, MIP, Funding Fee financed		If "Yes," complete question m below.				
o. Loan amount (add m & n)		m. Have you had an ownership interest in a property in the last three years?	☐	☐	☐	☐
		(1) What type of property did you own—principal residence (PR), second home (SH), or investment property (IP)?				
p. Cash from/to Borrower (subtract j, k, l & o from i)		(2) How did you hold title to the home—solely by yourself (S), jointly with your spouse (SP), or jointly with another person (O)?				

IX. ACKNOWLEDGMENT AND AGREEMENT

The undersigned specifically acknowledge(s) and agree(s) that: (1) the loan requested by this application will be secured by a first mortgage or deed of trust on the property described herein; (2) the property will not be used for any illegal or prohibited purpose or use; (3) all statements made in this application are made for the purpose of obtaining the loan indicated herein; (4) occupation of the property will be as indicated above; (5) verification or reverification of any information contained in the application may be made at any time by the Lender, its agents, successors and assigns, either directly or through a credit reporting agency, from any source named in this application, and the original copy of this application will be retained by the Lender, even if the loan is not approved; (6) the Lender, its agents, successors and assigns will rely on the information contained in the application and I/we have a continuing obligation to amend and/or supplement the information provided in this application if any of the material facts which I/we have represented herein should change prior to closing; (7) in the event my/our payments on the loan indicated in this application become delinquent, the Lender, its agents, successors and assigns, may, in addition to all their other rights and remedies, report my/our name(s) and account information to a credit reporting agency; (8) ownership of the loan may be transferred to successor or assign of the Lender without notice to me and/or the administration of the loan account may be transferred to an agent, successor or assign of the Lender with prior notice to me; (9) the Lender, its agents, successors and assigns make no representations or warranties, express or implied, to the Borrower(s) regarding the property, the condition of the property, or the value of the property.
Certification: I/We certify that the information provided in this application is true and correct as of the date set forth opposite my/our signature(s) on this application and acknowledge my/our understanding that any intentional or negligent misrepresentation(s) of the information contained in this application may result in civil liability and/or criminal penalties including, but not limited to, fine or imprisonment or both under the provisions of Title 18, United States Code, Section 1001, et seq. and liability for monetary damages to the Lender, its agents, successors and assigns, insurers and any other person who may suffer any loss due to reliance upon any misrepresentation which I/we have made on this application.

Borrower's Signature	Date	Co-Borrower's Signature	Date
X		X	

X. INFORMATION FOR GOVERNMENT MONITORING PURPOSES

The following information is requested by the Federal Government for certain types of loans related to a dwelling, in order to monitor the Lender's compliance with equal credit opportunity, fair housing and home mortgage disclosure laws. You are not required to furnish this information, but are encouraged to do so. The law provides that a Lender may neither discriminate on the basis of this information, nor on whether you choose to furnish it. However, if you choose not to furnish it, under Federal regulations this Lender is required to note race and sex on the basis of visual observation or surname. If you do not wish to furnish the above information, please check the box below. (Lender must review the above material to assure that the disclosures satisfy all requirements to which the Lender is subject under applicable state law for the particular type of loan applied for.)

BORROWER ☐ I do not wish to furnish this information

Race/National Origin: ☐ American Indian or Alaskan Native ☐ Asian or Pacific Islander ☐ White, not of Hispanic Origin ☐ Black, not of Hispanic origin ☐ Hispanic ☐ Other (specify) _____

Sex: ☐ Female ☐ Male

CO-BORROWER ☐ I do not wish to furnish this information

Race/National Origin: ☐ American Indian or Alaskan Native ☐ Asian or Pacific Islander ☐ White, not of Hispanic Origin ☐ Black, not of Hispanic origin ☐ Hispanic ☐ Other (specify) _____

Sex: ☐ Female ☐ Male

To be Completed by Interviewer	Interviewer's Name (print or type)	Name and Address of Interviewer's Employer
This application was taken by:		
☐ face-to-face interview	Interviewer's Signature Date	
☐ by mail		
☐ by telephone	Interviewer's Phone Number (incl. area code)	

Continuation Sheet/Residential Loan Application

Use this continuation sheet if you need more space to complete the Residential Loan Application. Mark B for Borrower or C for Co-Borrower.	Borrower:	Agency Case Number:
	Co-Borrower:	Lender Case Number:

APPENDIX 13

UNIFORM RESIDENTIAL APPRAISAL REPORT

[X] [X]

UNIFORM RESIDENTIAL APPRAISAL REPORT   File No.

SUBJECT / **Property Description**

Property Address	City	State / Zip Code
Legal Description		County
Assessor's Parcel No.	Tax Year / R.E. Taxes $	Special Assessments $
Borrower	Current Owner	Occupant [ ] Owner [ ] Tenant [ ] Vacant
Property rights appraised [ ] Fee Simple [ ] Leasehold	Project Type [ ] PUD [ ] Condominium (HUD/VA only)	HOA$ /Mo.
Neighborhood or Project Name	Map Reference	Census Tract
Sales Price $	Date of Sale	Description and $ amount of loan charges/concessions to be paid by seller
Lender/Client	Address	
Appraiser	Address	

NEIGHBORHOOD

Location	[ ] Urban	[ ] Suburban	[ ] Rural	Predominant occupancy	Single family housing PRICE $ (000) / AGE (yrs)	Present land use %	Land use change
Built up	[ ] Over 75%	[ ] 25-75%	[ ] Under 25%			One family	[ ] Not likely [ ] Likely
Growth rate	[ ] Rapid	[ ] Stable	[ ] Slow	[ ] Owner	Low	2-4 family	[ ] In process
Property values	[ ] Increasing	[ ] Stable	[ ] Declining	[ ] Tenant	High	Multi-family	To:
Demand/supply	[ ] Shortage	[ ] In balance	[ ] Over supply	[ ] Vacant (0-5%)	Predominant	Commercial	
Marketing time	[ ] Under 3 mos.	[ ] 3-6 mos.	[ ] Over 6 mos.	[ ] Vacant (over 5%)		( )	

Note: Race and the racial composition of the neighborhood are not appraisal factors.

Neighborhood boundaries and characteristics: _____

Factors that affect the marketability of the properties in the neighborhood (proximity to employment and amenities, employment stability, appeal to market, etc.): _____

Market conditions in the subject neighborhood (including support for the above conclusions related to the trend of property values, demand/supply, and marketing time - - such as data on competitive properties for sale in the neighborhood, description of the prevalence of sales and financing concessions, etc.): _____

PUD

Project information for PUDs (if applicable) - - Is the developer/builder in control of the Home Owners' Association (HOA)?   [ ] Yes   [ ] No

Approximate total number of units in the subject project _____   Approximate total number of units for sale in the subject project _____

Describe common elements and recreational facilities: _____

SITE

Dimensions _____		Topography _____
Site area _____	Corner Lot [ ] Yes [ ] No	Size _____
Specific zoning classification and description _____		Shape _____
Zoning compliance [ ] Legal [ ] Legal nonconforming (Grandfathered use) [ ] Illegal [ ] No zoning		Drainage _____
Highest & best use as improved [ ] Present use [ ] Other use (explain)		View _____

Utilities	Public	Other	Off-site Improvements	Type	Public	Private		
Electricity			Street				Landscaping	
Gas			Curb/gutter				Driveway Surface	
Water			Sidewalk				Apparent easements	
Sanitary sewer			Street lights				FEMA Special Flood Hazard Area [ ] Yes [ ] No	
Storm sewer			Alley				FEMA Zone _____ Map Date _____	
							FEMA Map No.	

Comments (apparent adverse easements, encroachments, special assessments, slide areas, illegal or legal nonconforming zoning use, etc.): _____

DESCRIPTION OF IMPROVEMENTS

GENERAL DESCRIPTION	EXTERIOR DESCRIPTION	FOUNDATION	BASEMENT	INSULATION
No. of Units	Foundation	Slab	Area Sq. Ft.	Roof [ ]
No. of Stories	Exterior Walls	Crawl Space	% Finished	Ceiling [ ]
Type (Det./Att.)	Roof Surface	Basement	Ceiling	Walls [ ]
Design (Style)	Gutters & Dwnspts.	Sump Pump	Walls	Floor [ ]
Existing/Proposed	Window Type	Dampness	Floor	None [ ]
Age (Yrs.)	Storm/Screens	Settlement	Outside Entry	Unknown [ ]
Effective Age (Yrs.)	Manufactured House	Infestation		

ROOMS	Foyer	Living	Dining	Kitchen	Den	Family Rm.	Rec. Rm.	Bedrooms	# Baths	Laundry	Other	Area Sq. Ft.
Basement												
Level 1												
Level 2												

Finished area above grade contains: Rooms;   Bedroom(s);   Bath(s);   Square Feet of Gross Living Area

INTERIOR	Materials/Condition	HEATING		KITCHEN EQUIP.		ATTIC		AMENITIES		CAR STORAGE:	
Floors		Type		Refrigerator		None [ ]		Fireplace(s) #		None [ ]	
Walls		Fuel		Range/Oven		Stairs [ ]		Patio		Garage	# of cars
Trim/Finish		Condition		Disposal		Drop Stair [ ]		Deck		Attached	
Bath Floor		COOLING		Dishwasher		Scuttle [ ]		Porch		Detached	
Bath Wainscot		Central		Fan/Hood		Floor [ ]		Fence		Built-in	
Doors		Other		Microwave		Heated [ ]		Pool		Carport	
		Condition		Washer/Dryer		Finished [ ]				Driveway	

COMMENTS

Additional features (special energy efficient items, etc.): _____

Condition of the improvements, depreciation (physical, functional, and external), repairs needed, quality of construction, remodeling/additions, etc.: _____

Adverse environmental conditions (such as, but not limited to, hazardous wastes, toxic substances, etc.) present in the improvements, on the site, or in the immediate vicinity of the subject property: _____

Freddie Mac Form 70 6-93   10 CH.   PAGE 1 OF 2   Fannie Mae Form 1004 6-93

Valuation Section   UNIFORM RESIDENTIAL APPRAISAL REPORT   File No.

COST APPROACH

ESTIMATED SITE VALUE. . . . . = $ _____
ESTIMATED REPRODUCTION COST-NEW OF IMPROVEMENTS:
Dwelling _____ Sq. Ft @ $ _____ = $ _____
_____ Sq. Ft @ $ _____ = _____
= _____
Garage/Carport _____ Sq. Ft @ $ _____ = $ _____
Total Estimated Cost-New . . . . = $ _____
Less   Physical | Functional | External
Depreciation _____ = $ _____
Depreciated Value of Improvements . . . . = $ _____
"As-is" Value of Site Improvements . . . . = $ _____
INDICATED VALUE BY COST APPROACH . . . . = $ _____

Comments on Cost Approach (such as, source of cost estimate, site value, square foot calculation and, for HUD, VA and FmHA, the estimated remaining economic life of the property): _____

SALES COMPARISON ANALYSIS

ITEM	SUBJECT	COMPARABLE NO. 1		COMPARABLE NO. 2		COMPARABLE NO. 3	
Address							
Proximity to Subject							
Sales Price	$		$		$		$
Price/Gross Liv. Area	$	☑ $		$		$	
Data and/or Verification Sources							
VALUE ADJUSTMENTS	DESCRIPTION	DESCRIPTION	+ (−) $ Adjustment	DESCRIPTION	+ (−) $ Adjustment	DESCRIPTION	+ (−) $ Adjustment
Sales or Financing Concessions							
Date of Sale/Time							
Location							
Leasehold/Fee Simple							
Site							
View							
Design and Appeal							
Quality of Construction							
Age							
Condition							
Above Grade	Total Bdrms Baths	Total Bdrms Baths		Total Bdrms Baths		Total Bdrms Baths	
Room Count							
Gross Living Area	Sq. Ft.	Sq. Ft.		Sq. Ft.		Sq. Ft.	
Basement & Finished Rooms Below Grade							
Functional Utility							
Heating/Cooling							
Energy Efficient Items							
Garage/Carport							
Porch, Patio, Deck, Fireplace(s), etc.							
Fence, Pool, etc.							
Net Adj. (total)		+ ☐ − ☐ $		+ ☐ − ☐ $		+ ☐ − ☐ $	
Adjusted Sales Price of Comparable		$		$		$	

Comments on Sales Comparison (including the subject property's compatibility to the neighborhood, etc.): _____

ITEM	SUBJECT	COMPARABLE NO. 1	COMPARABLE NO. 2	COMPARABLE NO. 3
Date, Price and Data Source for prior sales within year of appraisal				

Analysis of any current agreement of sale, option, or listing of the subject property and analysis of any prior sales of subject and comparables within one year of the date of appraisal: _____

INDICATED VALUE BY SALES COMPARISON APPROACH . . . . $ _____
INDICATED VALUE BY INCOME APPROACH (If Applicable) Estimated Market Rent $ _____ /Mo. x Gross Rent Multiplier _____ = $ _____
This appraisal is made ☐ "as is" ☐ subject to the repairs, alterations, inspections, or conditions listed below ☐ subject to completion per plans and specifications.
Conditions of Appraisal: _____

RECONCILIATION

Final Reconciliation: _____

The purpose of this appraisal is to estimate the market value of the real property that is the subject of this report, based on the above conditions and the certification, contingent and limiting conditions, and market value definition that are stated in the attached Freddie Mac Form 439/Fannie Mae Form 1004B (Revised _____).
I (WE) ESTIMATE THE MARKET VALUE, AS DEFINED, OF THE REAL PROPERTY THAT IS THE SUBJECT OF THIS REPORT, AS OF _____
(WHICH IS THE DATE OF INSPECTION AND THE EFFECTIVE DATE OF THIS REPORT) TO BE $ _____

APPRAISER:	SUPERVISORY APPRAISER (ONLY IF REQUIRED):	
Signature	Signature	☐ Did ☐ Did Not
Name	Name	Inspect Property
Date Report Signed	Date Report Signed	
State Certification # _____ State	State Certification # _____ State	
Or State License # _____ State	Or State License # _____ State	

Freddie Mac Form 70   6-93   10 CH.   PAGE 2 OF 2   Fannie Mae Form 1004   6-93

APPENDIX 14

PLAIN LANGUAGE MORTGAGE FORM[1]

MORTGAGE

WORDS USED OFTEN IN THIS DOCUMENT

(A) "Mortgage." This document, which is dated _____, 19__, will be called the "Mortgage."

(B) "Borrower." _____ will sometimes be called "Borrower" and sometimes simply "I."

(C) "Lender." _____ will be called "Lender." Lender is a corporation or association which was formed and which exists under the laws of _____. Lender's address is _____.

(D) "Note." The note signed by Borrower and dated _____ will be called the "Note." The Note shows that I owe Lender _____ Dollars plus interest, which I have promised to pay in monthly payments of principal and interest and to pay in full by _____.

(E) "Property." The property that is described below in the section titled "Description of the Property" will be called the "Property."

BORROWER'S TRANSFER TO LENDER OF RIGHTS IN THE PROPERTY

I mortgage, grant and convey the Property to Lender subject to the terms of this Mortgage. This means that, by signing this Mortgage, I am giving Lender those rights that are stated in this Mortgage and also that those rights that the law gives to lenders who hold mortgages on real property. I am giving Lender these rights to protect Lender from possible losses that might result if I fail to:

(A) Pay all the amounts that I owe Lender as stated in the Note;

(B) Pay, with interest, any amounts that Lender spends under this Mortgage, to protect the value of the Property and Lender's rights in the Property;

---

1   Designed by the Federal National Mortgage Association and the Federal Home Loan Mortgage Corporation.

(C) Pay, with interest, any other amounts that Lender lends to me as Future Advances under Paragraph 23 below; and

(D) Keep all of my other promises and agreements under this Mortgage

DESCRIPTION OF PROPERTY

I give Lender rights in the Property described in (A) through (J) below:

(A) The property which is located at _____
(Street)

_____, _____.
(City)   (State and Zip Code)

This property is in _____ County in the State of New York. It has the following legal description:

If this property is a condominium, the following must be completed: This property is part of a condominium project known as _____ (called the "Condominium Project"). This prop-
(Name of Condominium Project) erty includes my unit and all of my rights in the common elements of the Condominium Project.

If this property is in a planned unit development, the following must be completed: This property is in a development which is a planned unit development known as _____ (called the (Name of Planned Unit Development) "PUD"). The PUD was created by _____.
(Document Creating PUD)
(B) All buildings and other improvements that are located on the property described in paragraph (A) of this section;

(C) All rights in other property that I have as owner of the property described in paragraph (A) of this section. These rights are known as "easements, rights and appurtenances attached to the property";

(D) All rents or royalties from the property that I have described in paragraph (A) of this section. These rights in paragraph (A) of this section;

(E) All mineral, oil and gas rights and profits, water, water rights and water stock that are part of the property described in paragraph (A) of this section;

(F) All rights that I have in the land which lies in the streets or roads in front of, or next to, the property described in paragraph (A) of this section;

(G) All fixtures that are now or in the future will be on the property described in paragraphs (A) and (B) of this section, and all replacements of and additions to those fixtures, except for those "consumer goods" and that

quire more than ten days after the date of the Note. Usually, fixtures are physically attached to buildings, such as hot water heaters;

(H) All of the rights and property described in paragraphs (13) though (F) of this section that I acquire in the future;

(I) All replacements of or additions to the property described in paragraphs (13) through (F) and paragraph (H) of this section; and

(J) All of the amounts that I pay to Lender under Paragraph 2 below.

BORROWER'S RIGHT TO MORTGAGE THE PROPERTY AND BORROWER'S OBLIGATION TO DEFEND OWNERSHIP OF THE PROPERTY

I promise that except for the "exceptions" listed in any title insurance policy which insures Lender's rights in the Property: (A) I lawfully own the Property: (B) I have the right to mortgage, grant and convey the Property to Lender; and (C) there are no outstanding claims or charges against the Property.

I give a general warranty of title to Lender. This means that I will be fully responsible for any losses which Lender suffers because someone other than myself has some of the rights in the Property which I promise that I have. I promise that I will defend my ownership of the Property against any claims of such rights.

UNIFORM PROMISES

I promise and I agree with Lender as follows;

1. BORROWER'S PROMISE TO PAY PRINCIPAL AND INTEREST UNDER THE NOTE AND TO FULFILL OTHER PAYMENT OBLIGATIONS

I will promptly pay to Lender when due; principal and interest under the Note; late charges and prepayment charges as stated in the Note; and principal and interest on Future Advances that I may under Paragraph 23 below.

2. AGREEMENT ABOUT MONTHLY PAYMENT FOR TAXES AND INSURANCE

(A) Borrower's Obligation to Make Monthly Payments to Lender for Taxes and Insurance

I will pay to Lender all amounts necessary to pay for taxes, assessments, ground rents (if any), and hazard insurance on the Property and mortgage insurance (if any), I will pay those amounts to Lender unless Lender tells me, in writing that I do not have to do so, or unless the law requires otherwise. I will make those payments on the same day that my monthly payments of principal and interest are due under the Note.

The amount of each of my payments under this paragraph 2 will be the sum of the following:

(i) One-twelfth of the estimated yearly taxes, assessments and ground rents (if any) on the Property which under the law may be superior to this Property; plus

(ii) One-twelfth of the estimated yearly premium for hazard insurance covering the Property; plus

(iii) One-twelfth of the estimated yearly Premium for mortgage insurance (if any).

Lender will determine from time to time my estimated yearly taxes, assessments, ground rents and insurance premiums based upon existing assessments and bills, and estimates of future assessments and bills. (Taxes, assessments, ground rents and insurance premiums will be called "taxes and insurance.") The amounts that I pay to Lender for taxes and insurance under this Paragraph 2 will called the "Funds."

(B) Lender's Obligations Concerning Borrower's Monthly Payments for Taxes and Insurance

Lender will keep the Funds in a savings or banking institution which has its deposits or accounts insured or guaranteed by a Federal or state agency. If Lender is such an institution then lender may hold the Funds. Except as described in this Paragraph 2, Lender will use the Funds to pay taxes and insurance. Lender will give to me, without charge, an annual accounting of the Funds. That accounting must show all additions to and deductions from the Funds and the reason for each deduction. Lender may not charge me for holding or keeping the Funds on deposit, for using the Funds to pay taxes and insurance, for analyzing my payments of Funds, or for receiving, verifying and totaling assessments and bills. However, Lender may charge me for these services if Lender pays me interest on the Funds and if the law permits

Lender to make such a charge. Lender will not be required to pay me any interest or earnings on the Funds unless either (i) Lender and I agree in writing, at the time I sign this Mortgage, that Lender will pay interest on the Funds; or (ii) the law requires Lender to pay interest on the Funds. If Lender's estimates are too high or if taxes and insurance rates go down, the amounts that I pay under this Paragraph 2 will be too large. If this happens at a time when I am keeping all of my promises and agreements made in this Mortgage, I will have the right to have the excess amount either promptly repaid to me as a direct refund or credited to my future monthly pay the taxes and insurance when they are due.

If, when payments of taxes and insurance are due, Lender has not received enough Funds from me to make those payments, I will pay to Lender whatever additional amount is necessary to pay the taxes and insurance in full. I must pay that additional amount in one or more payments as Lender may require. When I have paid all of the amounts due under the Note and under this Mortgage, Lender will promptly refund to me any Funds that are then being held or kept on deposit by Lender under Paragraph 20 below either Lender acquire the Property or the Property is sold, then immediately before the acquisition or sale, Lender will use any Funds which Lender is holding or has on deposit at that time to reduce the amount that I owe to Lender under the Note and under this Mortgage.

3. LENDER'S APPLICATION OF BORROWER'S PAYMENTS

Unless the law requires otherwise, Lender will apply each of my payments under the Note and under Paragraphs I and 2 above in the following order and for the following purposes:

(A) First, to pay the amounts then due to Lender under Paragraph 2 above;

(B) Next, to pay interest then due under the Note;

(C) Next, to pay principal then due under the Note: and

(D) Next, to pay interest and principal on any Future Advances that I may have received from Lender under Paragraph 23 below.

4. BORROWER'S OBLIGATION TO PAY CHARGERS AND ASSESSMENTS AND TO SATISFY CLAIMS AGAINST THE PROPERTY

I will pay all taxes, assessments, and any other chargers and fines that may be imposed on the Property and that may be superior to this Mortgage. I will also make payments due under my lease of I am a tenant on the Property and I will pay ground rents (if any) due on the Property. I will do this either by making the payments to Lender that are described in Paragraph 2 above or, if I am not required to make payments under Paragraph 2. By making payments, when they are due, directly to the persons entitled to them. (In this Mortgage, the word "person" means any person, organization, governmental authority, or other party.) If I make direct payments, then promptly after making any of those payments I will give Lender a receipt which shows that I have done so. If I make payment to Lender under Paragraph 2, 1 will give Lender all notices or bills that I receive for the amounts due under this Paragraph 4.

Any claim, demand or charge that is made against property because an obligation has not been fulfilled is known as a "lien." I will promptly pay or satisfy all liens against the property that may be superior to this Mortgage. However, this Mortgage does not require me to satisfy a superior lien if: (A) I agree, in writing, to pay the obligation which gave rise to the superior lien and Lender approves the way in which I agree to pay that obligation; or (B) 1, in good faith, argue or defend against the superior lien in a lawsuit so that, during the lawsuit, the superior lien may not be enforced and no part of the Property must be given up.

Condominium and PUD Assessments

If the Property includes a unit in a Condominium Project or in a PUD, I will promptly pay, when they are due, all assessments imposed by the owners association or other organization that governs the Condominium Project or PUD. That Association or organization will be called the "Owners Association."

5. BORROWER'S OBLIGATION TO OBTAIN AND TO KEEP HAZARD INSURANCE ON THE PROPERTY

(A) Generally

I will obtain hazard insurance to cover all buildings and other improvements that now are or in the future will be located on the Property. The insurance must cover loss or damage caused by fire, hazards normally covered by "extended coverage" hazard insurance policies, and other hazards for which Lender requires coverage. The insurance must be in the amounts and for the periods of time required by Lender. It is possible that the insurance policy will have provisions that may limit the insurance company's obligation to pay claims if the amount of coverage is too low. Those provisions are known as "co-insurance requirements. Lender may not require me to obtain an amount of coverage that is more than the larger" larger of the following two amounts: either (1) the amount that I owe to Lender under the Note and under this Mortgage; or (ii) the amount necessary to satisfy the co-insurance requirements.

I may choose the insurance company, but my choice is subject to Lender's approval. Lender may not refuse to approve my choice unless the refusal is reasonable. All of the insurance policies and renewals of those policies must include what is known as a "standard mortgage clause" to protect Lender. The form of all policies and the form of all renewals must be acceptable to Lender. Lender will have the right to hold the policies and renewals.

I will pay the premiums on the insurance policies either by making payments to Lender, as described in Paragraph 2 above, or by paying the insurance company directly when the premium payments are due. If Lender requires, I will promptly give Lender all receipts of paid premiums and All renewal notices that I receive.

If there is a loss or damage to the Property, I will promptly notify the insurance company and Lender. If I do not promptly prove to the insurance company that the loss or damage occurred, then Lender may do so. The amount paid by the insurance company is called proceeds will be used to repair or to restore the damage Property unless: (a) it is not economically possible to make the repairs or restoration; or (b) the use of the proceeds for that purpose would lessen the protection given to Lender by this Mortgage; or (c) Lender and I have agreed in writing not to use the proceeds for that purpose. If the repair or restoration is not economically possible or if it would lessen Lender's protection under this Mortgage, then the proceeds will be used to reduce the amount that I owe to Lender under the Note and under this Mortgage. If any of the proceeds will be paid to me. The use of proceeds to reduce the amount that I owe to Lender will not be a prepayment that is subject to the prepayment that is subject to the prepayment charge provisions, if any, under the Note.

If I abandon the Property, or if I do not answer, within 30 days, a notice from Lender stating that the insurance company has offered to settle a claim for insurance benefits, then Lender has the authority to collect the proceeds. Lender may then use the proceeds to repair or restore the Property or to reduce the amount that I owe to Lender under the Note and under this Mortgage. The 30-day period will begin on the date the notice is mailed or, if it is not mailed, on the date the notice is delivered.

If any proceeds are used to reduce the amount of principal which I owe to Lender under the Note, that use will not delay the due date or change the amount of any of my monthly payments under the Note and under Paragraphs I and 2 above. However, Lender and I may agree in writing to those delays or changes.

If Lender acquires the Property under Paragraph 20 below, all of my rights in the insurance policies will belong to Lender. Also, all of my rights in any proceeds which are paid because of damage that occurred before the Property is acquired by Lender or sold will belong to Lender. However, Lender's rights in those proceeds will not be greater than the amount that I owe to Lender under the Note and under this Mortgage immediately before the Property is acquired by Lender or Sold.

(B) Agreements that Apply to Condominiums and PUD's

(i) If the Property includes a unit in a Condominium Project, the Owners Association may maintain a hazard insurance policy which covers the entire Condominium Project. That policy will be called the "master policy," So long as the master policy remains in effect and meets the requirements stated in this Paragraph 5: (a) my obligation to obtain and to keep hazard insurance on the Property is Satisfied; (b) I will not be required to include an amount for hazard insurance premiums in my monthly payment of Funds to Lender under Paragraph 2 above; and (c) if there is a conflict, concerning the use of proceeds, between (1) the terms of this Paragraph 5, and (2) the law or the terms of the declaration, by-laws, regulations or other documents creating or governing the Condominium Project, then that law or the terms of those documents will govern the use of proceeds. I will promptly give Lender notice if the master policy is interrupted or terminated. During any time that the master policy is not in effect the terrns of (a), (b) and (c) of this subparagraph 5(b) (i) will not apply.

(ii) If the Property includes a unit in a Condominium Project, it is possible that proceeds will be paid to me instead of being used to repair or to restore the Property. I give Lender my rights to those proceeds. If the Property includes a unit in a PUD, it is possible that precludes a unit in a PUD, it is possible that proceeds will be paid to me instead of being used to repair or to restore the Property. I give Lender my rights to those proceeds. If the Property includes a unit in a PUD, it is possible that proceeds will be paid to me instead of being used to repair or to restore the common areas or facilities of the PUD. I give Lender my rights to those proceeds. If the Property includes a unit in a PUD, it is possible that proceeds will be paid to me instead of being used to repair or to restore the common areas or facilities of the PUD. I give Lender my rights to those proceeds. All of the proceeds described in this subparagraph 5 (B)(ii) will be paid to Lender and will be used to reduce the amount that I owe to Lender under the Note and under this Mortgage. If any of those proceeds remain after the amount that I owe to Lender has been paid in full, the remaining proceeds will be paid to me. The use of proceeds to reduce the amount that I owe to Lender will not be a prepayment that is subject to the prepayment charge provisions, if any, under the Note.

6. BORROWER'S OBLIGATION TO MAINTAIN THE PROPERTY AND TO FULFILL OBLIGATIONS IN LEASE, AND AGREEMENTS ABOUT CONDOMINIUMS AND PUD'S

(A) Agreements about Maintaining the Property and Keeping Promises in Lease I will keep the Property in good repair. I will not destroy, damage or substantially change the Property, and I will not allow the Property to deteriorate. If do not own but am a tenant on the Property, I will fulfill my obligations under my lease.

(B) Agreements that Apply to Condominiums and PUD's If the Property is a unit in a Condominium Project or in a PUD, I will fulfill all of my obligations under the declaration, by-laws, regulations and other documents that create or govern the Condominium Project or PUD. Also, I will not divide the Property into smaller parts that may be owned separately (known as "partition or subdivision"). I will not consent to certain actions unless I have first given Lender notice and obtained Lenders's consent in writing. Those actions are:

(A) The abandonment or termination of the Condominium Project or PUD, unless, in the case of a condominium, the abandonment or termination is required by law;

(B) Any significant change to the declaration, by-laws or regulations of the Owners Association, trust agreement, articles of Incorporation, or other documents that create or govern the Condominium Project or PUD, including, for example, a change in the percentage of Ownership rights, held by unit owners, in the Condominium Project or in the common areas and facilities of the PUD;

(C) A Decision by the Owners Association to terminate professional management and to begin self-management of the Condominium Project or PUD; and

(D) The transfer, release, creation of liens, participation or subdivision of all or part of the common areas and facilities of the PUD. (How ever, this provision does not apply to the transfer by owners (However, this provision does not apply to the transfer by the Owners Association of rights to use those common areas and facilities for utilities and other similar or related purposes.)

7. LENDER'S RIGHT TO TAKE ACTION TO PROTECT THE PROPERTY

If:

(A) I do not keep my promises and agreement made in this Mortgage, or (B) someone, including me, begins a legal proceeding that may significantly affect Lender's rights in the Property (such as, for example, a legal proceeding in

8. LENDER'S RIGHT TO INSPECT THE PROPERTY

Lender, and others authorized by Lender, may enter on and inspect the Property. They must do so in a reasonable manner and at reasonable times. Before one of those inspections is made, Lender must give me notice stating a reasonable purpose for the inspection. That purpose must be related to Lender's rights in the Property.

9. AGREEMENTS ABOUT CONDEMNATION OF THE PROPERTY

A taking of property by any governmental authority by eminent domain is known as "condemnation." I give to Lender my right: (A) to proceeds of all awards or claims for damages resulting from condemnation or other governmen tal taking of the Property; and (B) to proceeds from a sale of the Property that is made to avoid condemnation. All of those proceeds will be paid to Lender.

If all of the Property is taken, the proceeds will be used to reduce the amount that I owe to Lender under the Note and under this Mortgage. If any of the proceeds remain after the amount that I owe to Lender has been paid in full, the remaining proceeds will be paid to me. Unless Lender and I agree otherwise in writing, if only a part of the Property is taken, the amount that I owe to Lender will only be reduced by the amount of proceeds multiplied by the following amount: (1) the total amount that I owe to Lender under the Note and under this Mortgage immediately before the taking, divided by (ii) the fair market value of the Property immediately before the taking, divided by (ii) the fair market value of the Property immediately before the taking. The remainder of the proceeds will be paid to me. The use of proceeds to reduce the amount that I owe to Lender will not be a prepayment that is subject to the prepayment charge provisions, if any, under the Note. If I abandon the Property, or if I do not answer, within 30 days, a notice from Lender stating that a governmental authority has offered to make a payment or to settle a claim for damages, then Lender has the authority to collect the proceeds.

Lender may then use the proceeds to repair or restore the Property or to reduce the amount that I owe to Lender under the Note and under this Mortgage. The 30-day period will begin on the date the notice is mailed or, if it is not mailed, on the date the notice is delivered. If any proceeds are used to reduce the amount of principal which I owe to Lender under the Note, that use will not delay the due date or change the amount of any of my monthly payments under the Note and under Paragraphs I and 2 above. However, Lender and I may agree in writing to those delays or changes. Condemnation of Common Areas of PUD

If the Property includes a unit in a PUD, the promises and agreements in this Paragraph 9 will apply to a condemnation, or sale to avoid condemnation, of the PUD's common areas and facilities as well as of the Property.

10. CONTINUATION OF BORROWER'S OBLIGATIONS

Lender may allow a person who takes over my rights and obligations to delay or to change the amount of the monthly payments of principal and interest due under the Note or under this Mortgage. Even if Lender does this, however, that person and I will both still be fully obligated under the Note and under this Mortgage unless the conditions stated in Paragraph 19 below have been met.

Lender may allow those delays or changes for a person who takes over my rights and obligations, even if Lender is requested not to do so. Lender will not be required to bring a lawsuit against such a person for not fulfilling obligations under the Note or under this Mortgage, even if Lender is requested to do so.

11. CONTINUATION OF LENDER'S RIGHTS

Even if Lender does not exercise or enforce any right of Lender under this Mortgage or under the law, Lender will still have all of those rights and may exercise and enforce them in the future. Even if Lender obtains insurance, pays taxes, or pays other claims, charges or liens against the Property, Lender will still have the right, under Paragraph 20 below, to demand that I make Immediate Payment In Full (see Paragraph 20 for a definition of this phrase) of the amount that I owe to Lender under the Note and under this Mortgage.

12. LENDER'S ABILITY TO ENFORCE MORE THAN ONE OF LENDER'S RIGHTS

Each of Lender's rights under this Mortgage is separate. Lender may exercise and enforce one or more of those rights, as well as any of Lender's other rights under the law, one at a time or all at once.

13. OBLIGATIONS OF BORROWERS AND OF PERSONS TAKING OVER BORROWER'S RIGHTS OR OBLIGATIONS; AGREEMENTS CONCERNING CAPTIONS

Subject to the terms of Paragraph 19 below, any person who takes over my rights or obligations under this Mortgage will have all of my rights and will be obligated to keep all of my promises and agreements made in this Mortgage. Similarly, any person who takes over Lender's rights or obligations under this Mortgage will have all of Lender's rights and will be obligated to keep all of Lender's agreements made in this Mortgage.

If more than one person signs this Mortgage as Borrower, each of us is fully obligated to keep all of Borrower's promises and obligations contained in this Mortgage. Lender may enforce Lender's rights under this Mortgage against each of us individually or against all of us together. This means that any one of us may be required to pay all of the amounts owed under the Note and under this Mortgage. However, if one of us does not sign the Note, then:

(A) that person is signing this Mortgage only to give that person's rights in the Property to Lender under the terms of this Mortgage; and

(B) that person is not personally obligated to make payments or to act under the Note or under this Mortgage.

The captions and titles of this Mortgage are for convenience only. They may not be used to interpret or to define the terms of this Mortgage.

14. AGREEMENTS ABOUT GIVING NOTICES REQUIRED UNDER THIS MORTGAGE

Unless the law requires otherwise, any notice that must be given to me under, this Mortgage will be given by delivering it or by mailing it addressed to me at the address stated in the section above titled "Description Of The Property." A notice will be delivered or mailed to me at a different address if I give Lender a notice of my different address. Any notice that must be given to Lender under this Mortgage will be given by mailing it to Lender's address stated in paragraph (C) of the section above titled 'Words Used Often In This Document." A notice will be mailed to Lender at a different address if Lender gives me a notice of the different address. A notice required by this Mortgage is given when it is mailed or when it is delivered according to the requirements of this Paragraph 14.

15. AGREEMENTS ABOUT UNIFORM MORTGAGE AND LAW THAT GOVERNS THIS MORTGAGE

This is a "Uniform Mortgage." It contains "uniform promises" that are in mortgages used all over the country and also "non-uniform promises" that vary, to a limited extent, in different parts of the country.

The law that applies in the place that the Property is located will govern this Mortgage. If any term of this Mortgage or of the Note conflicts with the law, all other terms of this Mortgage and of the Note will still remain in effect if they can be given effect without the conflicting term. This means than any terms of this Mortgage and of the Note which conflict with the law can be separated from the remaining terms, and the remaining terms will still be enforced.

16. BORROWER'S COPY OF THE NOTE AND OF THIS MORTGAGE

I will be given a copy of the Note and of this Mortgage. Those copies must show that the original Note and Mortgage have been signed. I will be given those copies either when I sign the Note and this Mortgage or after this Mortgage has been recorded in the proper official records.

17. AGREEMENTS THAT APPLY TO VA LOANS

A loan that is guaranteed or insured by the United States Veterans Administration is known as a "VA loan." If the loan that I promise to pay in the Note is a VA loan, then my rights and obligations, as well as those of Lender, are governed by that law which is known as Title 38 of the United States Code and the Regulations made under that Title (called the "VA Requirements"). One or more terms of this Mortgage, or of other documents that are signed in connection with my VA loan, might conflict with the VA Requirements. For example, the prepayment terms in the Note or Paragraph 19 of this Mortgage might conflict with the VA Requirements. Lender and I agree that if there is a conflict, the conflicting terms of this Mortgage or other documents are modified or eliminated as much as is necessary to make all of the conflicting terms agree with the VA Requirements.

gage insurance. I will pay the premiums until the requirement for mortgage insurance ends according to my written agreement with Lender or according to law. Lender may require me to pay the premiums in the manner described in Paragraph 2 above.

NON-UNIFORM PROMISES

I also promise and agree with Lender as follows:

19. AGREEMENTS ABOUT ASSUMPTION OF THIS MORTGAGE AND ABOUT LENDER'S RIGHTS IF BORROWER TRANSFERS THE PROPERTY WITHOUT MEETING CERTAIN CONDITIONS

If I sell or transfer all or part of the Property or any rights in the Property, any person to whom I sell or transfer the Property may take over all of my rights and obligations under this Mortgage (known as an "assumption of the Mortgage") if certain conditions are met. Those conditions are: (A) I give Lender notice of the sale or transfer; (B) Lender agrees that the person's credit is satisfactory; (C) the person agrees to pay interest on the amount owed to Lender under the Note and under this Mortgage at whatever rate Lender requires; and (D) the person signs an assumption agreement that is acceptable to Lender and that obligates the person to keep all of the promises and agreements made in the Note and in this Mortgage. If I sell or transfer the Property and each of the conditions in (A), (B), (C) and (D) of this Paragraph 19 is satisfied, Lender will release me from all of my obligations under the Note and under this Mortgage.

If I sell or transfer the Property and the conditions in (A), (B), (C) and (D) of this Paragraph 19 are not satisfied, I will still be fully obligated under the Note and under this Mortgage and Lender may require Immediate Payment In Full, as that phrase is defined in Paragraph 20 below. However, Lender will not have the right to require Immediate Payment In Full as a result of certain transfers. Those transfers are: (i) the creation of liens or other claims against the Property that are inferior to this Mortgage; (ii) a transfer of rights in household appliances, to a person who provides me with the money to buy those appliances, in order to protect that person against possible losses; (iii) a transfer of the Property to surviving co-owners, following the death of a co-owner, when the transfer is automatic according to law; (iv) leasing the Property for a term of three years or less, as long as the lease does not include an option to buy.

If Lender requires Immediate Payment In Full under this Paragraph 19, Lender will send me, in the manner described in Paragraph 14 above, a notice which states this requirement. The notice will give me at least 30 days to make the required payment. The 30-day period will begin on the date the notice is mailed or, if it is not mailed, on the date the notice is delivered. If I do not make the required payment during that period, Lender may bring a lawsuit for "foreclosure and sale" under Paragraph 20 below without giving me any further notice or demand for payment. (See Paragraph 20 for a definition of "foreclosure and sale.")

20. LENDER'S RIGHTS IF BORROWER FAILS TO KEEP PROMISES AND AGREEMENTS

If all of the conditions stated in subparagraphs (A), (B), and (C) of this Paragraph 20 are met, Lender may require that I pay immediately the entire amount then remaining unpaid under the Note and under this Mortgage. Lender may do this without making any further demand for payment. This requirement will be called "Immediate Payment in Full."

If Lender requires Immediate Payment In Full, Lender may bring a lawsuit to take away all of my remaining rights in the Property and to have the Property sold. At this sale Lender or another person may acquire the Property. This is known as "foreclosure and sale." In any lawsuit for foreclosure and sale, Lender will have the right to collect all costs allowed by law.

Lender may require Immediate Payment In Full under this Paragraph 20 only if all of the following conditions are met:

(A) I fall to keep any promise or agreement made in this Mortgage, including the promises to pay when due the amounts that I owe to Lender under the Note and under this Mortgage; and

(B) Lender sends to me, in the manner described in Paragraph 14 above, a notice that states:

(i) The promise or agreement that I failed to keep;

(ii) The action that I must take to correct that failure;

(iii) A date by which I must correct the failure. That date must be at least 30 days from the date on which the notice is mailed to me, or, if it is not mailed, from the date on which it is delivered to me;

(iv) That if I do not correct the failure by the date stated in the notice, I will be in default and Lender may require Immediate Payment In Full, and Lender or another person may acquire the Property by means of foreclosure and sale;

(v) That I may speak with a named representative of Lender to discuss any questions which I have about the things stated in the notice;

(vi) That if I meet the conditions stated in Paragraph 21 below, I will have the right to have any lawsuit for foreclosure and sale discontinued and to have the Note and this Mortgage remain in full effect as if Immediate Payment In Full had never been required; and

(vii) That I have the right in any lawsuit for foreclosure and sale to argue that I did keep my promises and agreements under the Note and under this Mortgage, and to present any other defenses that I may have; and

(C) I do not correct the failure stated in the notice from Lender by the date stated in that notice.

21. BORROWER'S RIGHT TO HAVE LENDER'S LAWSUIT FOR FORECLOSURE AND SALE DISCONTINUED

Even if Lender has required Immediate Payment In Full, I may have the right to have discontinued any lawsuit brought by Lender for foreclosure and sale or for other enforcement of this Mortgage. I will have this right at any time before a judgment has been entered enforcing this Mortgage if I meet the following conditions:

(A) I pay to Lender the full amount that would have been due under this Mortgage, the Note, and any notes for Future Advances under Paragraph 23 below if Lender had not required Immediate Payment In Full; and

(B) I correct my failure to keep any of my other promises or agreements made in this Mortgage; and

(C) I pay all of Lender's reasonable expenses in enforcing this Mortgage including, for example, reasonable attorney's fees; and

(D) I do whatever Lender reasonably requires to assure that Lender's rights in the Property, Lender's rights under this Mortgage, and my obligations under the Note and under this Mortgage continue unchanged.

If I fulfill all of the conditions in this Paragraph 21, then the Note and this Mortgage will remain in full effect as if Immediate Payment In Full had never been required.

22. LENDER'S RIGHTS TO RENTAL PAYMENTS FROM THE PROPERTY AND TO TAKE POSSESSION OF THE PROPERTY

As additional protection for Lender, I give to Lender all of my rights to any rental payments from the Property. However, until Lender requires Immediate Payment In Full under Paragraphs 19 or 20 above, or until I abandon the Property, I have the right to collect and keep those rental payments as they become due. I have not given any of my rights to rental payments from the Property to anyone else, and I will not do so without Lender's consent in writing.

If Lender requires Immediate Payment In Full under Paragraph 19 or 20 above, or if I abandon the Property, then Lender, persons authorized by Lender, or a receiver appointed by a court at Lender's request may: (A) collect the rental payments, including overdue rental payments, directly from the tenants; (B) enter on and take possession of the Property; (C) manage the Property; and (D) sign, cancel and change leases. I agree that if Lender notifies the tenants that Lender has the right to collect rental payments directly from them under this Paragraph 22, the tenants may make those rental payments to Lender without having to ask whether I have failed to keep my promises and agreements under this Mortgage.

If there is a judgment for Lender in a lawsuit for foreclosure and sale, I will pay to Lender reasonable rent from the date the judgment is entered for as long as I occupy the Property. However, this does not give me the right to occupy the Property.

All rental payments collected by Lender or by a receiver, other than the rent paid by me under this Paragraph 22, will be used first to pay the costs of collecting rental payments and of managing the Property. If any part of the rental payments remains after those costs, have been paid in full, the remaining part will be used to reduce the amount that I owe to Lender under the Note and under this Mortgage. The costs of managing the Property may include the receiver's fees reasonable attorney's fees, and the cost of any necessary bonds. Lender and the receiver will be obligated to account only for those rental payments that they actually receive.

23. AGREEMENTS ABOUT FUTURE ADVANCES

I may ask Lender to make one or more loans to me in addition to the loan that I promise to pay under the Note. Lender may, before this Mortgage is discharged, make those additional loans to me. This Mortgage will protect Lender from possible losses that might result from any failure to pay the amounts of any of those additional loans plus interest, only if the notes which contain my promises to pay those additional loans state that this Mortgage will give Lender such protection. Additional loans made by Lender that are protected by this Mortgage will be called "Future Advances." The principal amount that I owe to Lender under the Note and under all notes for Future Advances, not including the amounts spent by Lender to protect the value of the

Property and Lender's rights in the Property, may not be greater than the original amount of the Note plus US $_____.

24. LENDER'S OBLIGATION TO DISCHARGE THIS MORTGAGE WHEN THE NOTE AND THIS MORTGAGE ARE PAID IN FULL

When Lender has been paid all amounts due under the Note, under this Mortgage and under any notes for Future Advances, Lender will discharge this Mortgage by delivering a certificate stating that this Mortgage has been satisfied. I will not be required to pay Lender for the discharge, but I will pay all costs of recording the discharge in the proper official records.

25. AGREEMENTS ABOUT NEW YORK LIEN LAW

I will receive all amounts lent to me by Lender subject to the trust fund provisions of Section 13 of the New York Lien Law. This means that if, on the date this Mortgage is recorded in the proper official records, construction or other work on any building or other improvement located on the Property has not been completed for at least four months, I will: (A) hold all amounts, which I receive and which I have a right to receive from Lender under the Note and as Future Advances, as a "trust fund"; and (B) use those amounts to pay for that construction or work before I use them for any other purpose. The fact that I am holding those amounts as a "trust fund" means that I have a special responsibility under the law to use the amounts in the manner described in this paragraph 25.

By signing this mortgage I agree to all of the above.
Witnesses:

_____   _____
                                                          Borrower

_____   _____
                                                          Borrower

State of New York,_____County ss:

On this _____ day of _____19_____, before me personally came_____to me known and known to me to be the individual(s) described in and who executed the foregoing instrument, and _he_ dully acknowledged to me that _he_ executed the same.

                              _____
                                        Notary Public

APPENDIX 15

MORTGAGE NOTE

The undersigned Maker [whether one or more] promises to pay to the order of [Name] of [Address] the principal sum of [$ Principal Amount] in [#] equal installments of [$ Payment Amount] payable on [monthly payment date] and on the same day of each month thereafter, PLUS a final payment of unpaid principal balance and accrued interest due on [final payment date].

All payments include principal and interest. This Note bears Interest on the unpaid balance before maturity at the rate of [xx%] per year. All unpaid principal and accrued interest shall bear interest after maturity of this Note, whether occurring through lapse of time or acceleration at the rate of [xx%] per year until paid.

In any installment of principal and interest is not paid on or before the 10th day after its due date, Holder may collect a delinquency charge at the rate of [xx%] per year on the amount of the installment from the due date until paid or until maturity, whichever is earlier.

This Note is secured by a real estate mortgage dated [Date of Mortgage] from [Name] to the payee. If Maker fails to make a payment under this Note when due, and the default continues for 10 days, or upon the occurrence of an event of default described in the mortgage or any other agreement securing this Note, the Holder may declare the entire balance of principal and accrued interest to be payable immediately without notice or demand. All payments shall be applied in such manner as the Holder determines to interest, principal and payments due under the mortgage. At any time after the occurrence of an event of default, Holder may apply any credit balance or other money at any time owed by Holder to Maker, to all or any part of the unpaid balance of this Note.

All Makers, endorsers, sureties and guarantors agree to pay all costs of collection, including the extent not prohibited by law, reasonable attorney's fees.

If checked here, any installment paid within [#] days not to exceed 30 days prior to or after the due date shall include interest to the due date of the installment and no delinquency charge will be imposed on that installment.

If checked here, this Note may otherwise be prepaid in full or in part without penalty, and if prepaid in full, unearned interest, if any will be refunded to the extent required by law.

If checked here, full or partial prepayment of this Note: [Describe prepayment restrictions and penalty, if any]

Presentment, demand and notice of dishonor are waived.

Without affecting the liability of any Maker, Endorser, surety or guarantor, the Holder may, without notice, grant renewals or extensions, accept partial payments, release or impair any collateral security for the payment of this Note, or agree not to sue any party liable on it.

Maker acknowledges receipt of any exact copy of this Note.

[Signature Line-Address-Date]

[Signature Line-Address-Date]

[Signature Line-Address-Date]